estherpress

Books for Courageous Women

ESTHER PRESS VISION

*Publishing diverse voices that encourage and equip women to walk
courageously in the light of God's truth for such a time as this.*

BIBLICAL STATEMENT OF PURPOSE

*"For if you keep silent at this time, relief and deliverance will rise for the Jews from
another place, but you and your father's house will perish. And who knows whether
you have not come to the kingdom for such a time as this?"*

Esther 4:14 (ESV)

What people are saying about …

IMAGE RESTORED

"This is a message that women have needed. Rachael tackles a topic many of us struggle with but no one really talks about. What a transformative and grace-filled message on overcoming the lies we believe about our bodies and replacing them with God's truth!"

Amy Ford, president of Embrace Grace, author of *Help Her Be Brave*

"A must-read for anyone struggling with body image or identity. Rachael artfully brings together personal experience, clinical expertise, and spiritual truths for a winning combination. Her honest stories welcome the reader through healing's open door. She provides the practical guidance of a professional counselor's voice and the gentle invitation to measure beliefs against the plumbline of God's Word. Rachael's creative approach makes for an interactive and pleasurable therapeutic experience."

Linda Hoover, PsyD, clinical psychologist and Executive Dean of Academics at the King's University

"Every woman has struggled with body image issues, but not every woman has a wise, insightful, encouraging, and authentic guide to help her. That's exactly what you'll get with Rachael Gilbert. Her words are an echo of the heart of the Creator, who deeply loves and intentionally designed every part of you."

Holley Gerth, *Wall Street Journal*–bestselling author of *What Your Mind Needs for Anxious Moments*

"*Image RESTored* offers readers an incredibly clear and thorough blueprint for overcoming body image issues. Rachael writes with the knowledge and expertise of a therapist and the compassion and vulnerability of a dear friend. This resource is chock-full of real-life stories, therapeutic insights, practical tips, applicable Scripture, and so much more. It is a must-read for anyone desiring to be free from the bondage of body image insecurities."

Ashley Willis, author of *Peace Pirates*

"The church needs more books that teach you how to live out your faith through your body—an embodied faith. The enemy of joy and freedom would like to keep you stuck in a cycle of obsessing over and neglecting your body, never free to glorify God with it. Rachael helps you break free from that fruitless cycle, working with you until how you see your body mirrors how God sees you. After working through this book, your body home will be built on the Rock."

Alisa Keeton, founder of Revelation Wellness, author of
The Wellness Revelation and *Heir To the Crown*

"Rachael has written a delightful guide for every Christian woman who wants to finally replace the lies she believes about her body with truth from God's Word. She writes like a friend who is cheering you on. But make no mistake— you're reading well-researched wisdom from a counselor who is trained to help you!"

Dannah Gresh, founder of True Girl, bestselling author

"Body image struggles are so much more than a body issue—and finally, there's a book that tells the whole story. Inside these pages, Rachael pulls from her love for the Lord, her training as a counselor, and her experience as a woman who has been there to weave together a beautiful combination of God's truth, personal reflection, and practical application. If you struggle to see yourself how God sees you, this is the conversation for you."

Michelle Myers, cofounder of She Works His Way and
author of the Conversational Commentary series

"For the Christian woman struggling with body shame, author Rachael Gilbert has a message of freedom for you: *Your body is good*. In a creative integration of spiritual and psychological principles, Rachael shares the real stories that convince you of this truth. *Image RESTored* will positively change your relationship with your body—and yourself—and the God who beautifully designed you."

Amy O'Hana, PhD, licensed professional
counselor and author of *Beyond Burnout*

"If perfectionism has ever influenced your self-image, this book offers relief and hope. Rachael unravels the mysteries of shame, guilt, hidden hurts, and unresolved trauma as they relate to body image. She captures the nuances of self-awareness and recovery while providing a road map for healing the soul. Rachael's skilled and informative approach as a licensed mental health professional offers a safe place for finding healing."

Mary Dainty, PhD, LPC-S, private practitioner and counselor
supervisor, adjunct faculty at the King's University

"What a refreshing, powerfully written book of thought-provoking insights providing practical applications that can be used right away. I love the conceptualizations for the counselor and the strategies of how to navigate those client dynamics effectively."

Shannan Crawford, PsyD, licensed psychologist, podcast
host of *Unlock U with Dr. Shannan Crawford*

"I'm so glad you picked up this book. I doubt if you've read a more transparent and unfiltered book that is sure to change the way you think. From the very first pages, my longtime friend Rachael Gilbert wastes no time reading your mail and challenging your thinking. If you need your *image restored*, this spiritually accurate yet profoundly practical book will give you a perfect blueprint to construct a healthy picture of who you are in Christ. What are you waiting for? Start reading it today!"

Jon Chasteen, EdD, president of the King's University & Seminary,
senior pastor of Victory Church, author of *Half the Battle*

IMAGE RESTORED

TEAR DOWN SHAME AND INSECURITY TO EXPERIENCE A BODY IMAGE RENOVATION

RACHAEL GILBERT

estherpress

Books for Courageous Women
from David C Cook

IMAGE RESTORED
Published by Esther Press
An Imprint of David C Cook
4050 Lee Vance Drive
Colorado Springs, CO 80918 U.S.A.

Integrity Music Limited, a Division of David C Cook
Brighton, East Sussex BN1 2RE, England

Esther Press, David C Cook, and related logos are trademarks of David C Cook.

The website addresses recommended throughout this book are offered as a resource to you. These websites are not intended in any way to be or imply an endorsement on the part of David C Cook, nor do we vouch for their content.

Unless otherwise noted, all Scripture quotations are taken from the Holy Bible, New International Version®, NIV®. Copyright © 1973, 2011 by Biblica, Inc.™ Used by permission of Zondervan. All rights reserved worldwide. www.zondervan.com. The "NIV" and "New International Version" are trademarks registered in the United States Patent and Trademark Office by Biblica, Inc.™ Scripture quotations marked ESV are taken from the ESV® Bible (The Holy Bible, English Standard Version®), copyright © 2001 by Crossway, a publishing ministry of Good News Publishers. Used by permission. All rights reserved. MSG are taken from THE MESSAGE, copyright © 1993, 2018 by Eugene H. Peterson. Used by permission of NavPress, represented by Tyndale House Publishers. All rights reserved; NASB are taken from the (NASB®) New American Standard Bible®, Copyright © 1960, 2020 by The Lockman Foundation. Used by permission. All rights reserved. www.lockman.org; NLT are taken from the Holy Bible, New Living Translation, copyright © 1996, 2015 by Tyndale House Foundation. Used by permission of Tyndale House Publishers, Carol Stream, Illinois 60188. All rights reserved. The author has added italics to Scripture quotations for emphasis.

ISBN 978-0-8307-8289-5
eISBN 978-0-8307-8290-1

© 2023 First Fruit Fitness, LLC

The Team: Susan McPherson, Stephanie Bennett, Julie Cantrell, Judy Gillispie, Renée Chavez, James Hershberger, Susan Murdock
Cover Design: James Hershberger
Cover Images: Creative Market

Printed in the United States of America
First Edition 2023

1 2 3 4 5 6 7 8 9 10

110322

To Matt,

for loving me as Christ loves the church. You have been the hands and feet of Jesus on my journey to healing and writing this book. Thank you for being my rock. I love you with all my heart, forever and always, no matter what.

Contents

Foreword by Robert Morris   13

Introduction: An Inside-Out Approach to Body Image   15

Unit 1: The Foundation

Chapter 1: Choose a Building Site   25

Chapter 2: Cracks in the Foundation   35

Chapter 3: The Original Design   45

Unit 1 Counselor's Cornerstone   55

Unit 2: The Floor Plan

Chapter 4: Structural Stories   61

Chapter 5: If Walls Could Talk   71

Chapter 6: Hidden Hurt in the Closet   81

Unit 2 Counselor's Cornerstone   91

Unit 3: The Framework

Chapter 7: Thoughts Are the Foreman   97

Chapter 8: The Creaky Floorboards   107

Chapter 9: When Building Is Delayed   117

Unit 3 Counselor's Cornerstone   127

Unit 4: The Interior

Chapter 10: Decorating with Idols   133

Chapter 11: The House Next Door   143

Chapter 12: Moldy Motives   155

Unit 4 Counselor's Cornerstone   163

Unit 5: The Exterior

Chapter 13: Curb Appeal and Being Real   169

Chapter 14: Break the Alarm Cycle   179

Chapter 15: The Only One on the Block   189

Unit 5 Counselor's Cornerstone   199

Unit 6: The Covering

Chapter 16: God's Love and Jesus' Blood   205

Chapter 17: God's Grace and Jesus' Face   215

Chapter 18: Find Your Body Image Neighborhood   225

Unit 6 Counselor's Cornerstone   237

Afterword: The Final Walk-Through   241

Acknowledgments   247

Notes   251

Resources   253

Foreword

Years ago, God gave me a burden to teach the church about biblical stewardship, and much of my ministry has been devoted to that calling. My wife, Debbie, and I wanted to model for our church a kind of generosity that would inspire people to become extravagant givers, and through that we have seen God do amazing things!

However, as Gateway Church grew, God asked me a question about my own giving that I wasn't prepared for. He asked if I would give Him the most extravagant offering I could possibly give. He asked if I would give Him my body. What He meant by this was a commitment to eating right and exercising. I asked if I could just give Him an extra 10 percent of my finances instead, because a healthy diet and daily exercise have been areas of weakness in my life for a long time. (He said no, by the way!)

That's why this book connected so deeply with me. For years, I had an incorrect view of my health and tried to take an outside-in approach through various diets. In fact, I joke that I have probably lost seven hundred pounds in my adult life! But the diets never seemed to have a lasting effect. That's because I was doing them for all the wrong reasons. I was focused *first* on improving my outward appearance, but the truth is that it was all related to my pride. I had to work on the inside first. And that's what is so great about this book—it focuses on an inside-out approach built on a biblical foundation.

I am so proud of Rachael and the work she's put into this book. I love how she mixes real-life experience with a biblical worldview and the expertise of a therapist. Rachael earned her master of Marriage and Family degree at the King's University and is a licensed counselor. Throughout the book she shares Therapist Thoughts, which give context and a therapist's perspective to each chapter. But more than anything, it's Rachael's stories that bring the lessons in this book to life. Through her stories, you can see how the Enemy tries to use body image as one of his primary targets. Is there a struggle more universal than the one surrounding our views of our own bodies? Satan knows this is an easy target, and frankly, it's one that is not discussed very often in the church. That's why I am so glad Rachael wrote this book and shined a bright light on this subject. As you read her stories, you're sure to recognize similarities in your own journey. You'll also be given a path to freedom and a framework for rebuilding your body image from the inside out.

Rebuilding is actually the primary theme of the book. In some sections, you'll read about tearing down false beliefs, and in others you'll read how to carefully rebuild with truth. You'll also realize that the rebuilding process is ongoing, and as you grow closer to God, you'll find more areas of your life in need of renovation. I believe there is such a need for this book in the church right now, and there's no better person to write it than Rachael.

Years ago, when my nephew Matthew introduced Debbie and me to Rachael, his wife-to-be, we knew she was someone special and that he had made a great choice. Little did we know our first impression would prove correct many times over! We have seen the fruit of what Rachael teaches in the way she lives, and we wholeheartedly recommend her and her book.

I am confident that as you read these words with a heart open to hear what the Holy Spirit says, you'll experience a tremendous change in your life and experience a great breakthrough.

Robert Morris
senior pastor of Gateway Church,
bestselling author of *The Blessed Life*,
The God I Never Knew, Beyond Blessed,
and *Take the Day Off*

An Inside-Out Approach to Body Image

Do you like the way your body looks? If you're like most women, you'd probably say no. And guess what? I've felt the same struggles most of my life. I've lost track of the number of times I've stared in the mirror and wished my body was thinner ... more toned ... less curvy ... just DIFFERENT!

Have you ever felt ashamed of your body? *In college, I had a season during which I wouldn't leave my apartment because I was ashamed of my weight gain.*

Have you ever left a beauty treatment feeling more disappointed than when you arrived? *I can't even count how many stylists have accidentally dyed my hair black in a salon.*

Do you bounce up and down with the yo-yo of dieting and bingeing? *I have bounced so many times that for years I owned a spectrum of pant sizes ranging from single to double digits.*

As a "good Christian girl," I long believed I shouldn't struggle with these issues. I wondered what was wrong with me. Perhaps you've felt this way too?

If so, I'm sorry you know this struggle, but I'm also glad you're here among women who understand. If you've ever faced insecurities about your body, I've written this book for you. Thank you for trusting me to be both your friend and your guide as I walk beside you on your path to healing and wholeness.

We're All in This Together

While working toward my master's degree in marriage and family therapy, I was assigned to write a six-week curriculum that could be used for group counseling. I chose to research the topic of body image, an issue that had become a huge part of my life. While I felt called to serve women who struggle in this area, I was also looking for answers myself.

To complete this project, I conducted a ten-question survey with 138 women, ages twenty-two to seventy-six, who identified as Christian. The responses were staggering.

When asked, "Do you like the way your body looks?" 99.98 percent of the women responded no. The few who said yes followed up with a statement such as, "… but I wish I could get back to my pre-baby body," "… I wish I could flatten out my tummy," "… I wish I could get rid of this cellulite."

Sadly, I could fill this entire book discussing the many ways these women *wished* they could change their bodies.

When these same women were asked, "Do you believe you were made in God's image?" 99 percent answered yes, but most followed it with a statement like, "I know it in my head, but I want to feel it in my heart."

As I read their responses, tears filled my eyes because I had felt many of these same insecurities regarding my own physical appearance. Then I read the responses to another question: "Have you ever hidden your body image struggles or disordered diet behaviors from others?"

The answer to this question was 100 percent YES.

These results hit me particularly hard because I, too, had spent most of my life hiding my body image struggles from others. I pictured each of these women battling her insecurities alone, and I realized we had all been taking the same painful journey … all while feeling as if we were the only ones navigating that path.

While the survey I conducted was eye opening, I knew my small study of 138 women wasn't enough. I went on a quest to find more clinical research, and to be honest, there wasn't much to be found. Why? Because historically, there hasn't been enough funding directed toward body dysmorphia and eating disorders.

Thankfully, things are shifting in this area of research, but we still have a long way to go. While scientists are working to understand the rise in eating disorders—and though our culture continues to place increasing pressures on women regarding body image—we can rest assured that God is not surprised or overwhelmed by this growing issue.

In fact, I was thrilled to find a study that researched attachment to God and its effects on body satisfaction. According to Exline and Kussina, findings revealed that a more secure "perceived attachment to God" was associated with more body appreciation.[1]

Friends, what you just read is huge. Scientists admitted that a secure attachment to God can improve body image!

> Scientists admitted that a secure attachment to God can improve body image!

Likewise, if we aren't planted on a firm spiritual foundation, no amount of weight loss, surgical intervention, or beauty treatments will change how we see our bodies. I'm betting we've all tried an outside-in approach by attempting to fix the outside of our bodies, with little-to-no lasting change on our internal body image. That's why we're about to embrace an inside-out approach to restoring body image.

In this book, we'll debunk what we've learned about our bodies and replace it with a secure attachment to our Creator.

The Time Is Now

The same survey I conducted for my graduate research also asked the participating women how old they were when they first began having an issue with their bodies. The ages varied, but most women reported being under ten years old when they first felt that struggle. The average participant was between thirty and forty at the time of the study, which suggests these women had been alone in a body image battle for two to three decades. My heart ached to think of how many moments they'd missed out on in life because of body shame.

In my private practice as a licensed professional counselor associate, it is rare that I meet a woman who has not faced at least a few body image battles. For most women, it is not a question of *if* we will struggle with this issue but *when*. New seasons bring new challenges, especially when it comes to our aging and ever-changing bodies. This struggle is nothing to be ashamed of, yet we carry it on our shoulders in private, perhaps feeling as if there's no safe space to share our deepest fears.

I can't think of a better way to walk this journey than with friends who are in the trenches with us. That's why I think of this book as more than just a message; it's a movement. As we work though this healing process, I hope you'll join me in inspiring women of every shape and size to reclaim their body confidence and live life to the fullest, just as God intended us to do. No shame allowed!

Walk with Me

If you're feeling hesitant to share your body image issues with others, I understand. I was a sophomore in college when I told my small group leader at church about my struggles. It was the first time I'd told anyone about my body issues, and I could tell by the stunned look on her face that she was ready to call someone for help. I quickly assured her that I had found my way to freedom and was just offering a testimony of what I had already overcome.

Much to my surprise, the next week, I received a phone call from my college pastor. He let me know that the leader had shared my "testimony" with him and that he would like me to share it with my college peers—nearly a thousand students! In my head, I was screaming, *Nope, nope, nope … Can't you all see I am STILL in this struggle?!*

I managed to politely decline by letting him know I was not a public speaker. He told me to pray about it, to which I agreed, but I never did bring the topic up to God. Instead, I dodged my campus pastor and life group leader that entire semester for fear they would somehow wrestle me down and hand me a microphone.

Here's the truth: I have dodged this call to write and speak on this topic of body image for far too long. While I probably was not in the best place to share in college (especially since I was still in the thick of the struggle), I can't help but wonder who else would have stood up in that auditorium and said, "I struggle too."

Now, almost twenty years later, I am finally ready to share what I've learned, not only from my walk with God but also from my education and training. I earned my undergraduate degree in exercise physiology, my master of marriage and family therapy, and my license as a professional counselor (LPC Associate). I've also partnered with my husband, Matt (a doctor of chiropractic), in our family-owned business, the BBC Health, where we offer an integrated team approach to health care. While I don't expect you to be impressed with my credentials, I want you to understand the huge role this theme of body image plays in my life and how much time and energy I've devoted to helping others, like you, find their way to freedom.

The Vision for the Restored Body Image House

In counseling women who struggle with body image, I have noticed that, much like grief, body image healing does not follow an exact formula or timeline. When God called me to write a book on what I've learned, I wasn't sure where to begin. The truth is, there are many layers to healing from an unhealthy body image. Even when I'm invited to speak on body image, I usually have time to address only one aspect of the broader issue. I liken it to giving someone a single piece of a puzzle and expecting her to complete the whole picture.

God's timing in life never ceases to amaze me, because as I set out to pull together a cohesive book on body image, Matt and I also began building a new home. As the architect walked us through the many steps of the process, the Lord showed me that He wanted me to take the same approach with this book. He impressed upon my heart that He wants to *restore* this territory the Enemy has wreaked havoc in for far too long. It starts with rebuilding our image from the ground up.

Much as with building a home, we must first envision what we hope to have when the work is finished. The architect delivered a picture of what our home would look like upon completion, and I want you to picture what your life will look like when you complete your healing journey. Ultimately, we want your end result to be FREEDOM.

Just as a construction project encounters various delays, stalls, and problems, the journey to healing may face interruptions. Each woman will complete the journey in her *own* time. For that reason, I can't promise your freedom will come all at once. But I can guarantee the Lord will bring more peace and healing with each step you take in the right direction.

Along the way, I want you to treat this book as your body image diary. That's why I've laid it out in such a way that you'll get a chance to read, write, complete exercises, and even color within these pages.

The eighteen chapters are divided into six key units based on the Image Restored Blueprint:

1. The Foundation
2. The Floor Plan
3. The Framework
4. The Interior
5. The Exterior
6. The Covering

IMAGE RESTORED

THE COVERING
LOVE · GRACE · COMMUNITY

THE EXTERIOR
EXPECTATIONS · HABITS · UNIQUE PURPOSE

THE INTERIOR
IDOLS · COMPARISON · MOTIVES

THE FRAMEWORK
THOUGHTS · FEELINGS · BEHAVIORS

THE FLOOR PLAN
YOUR STORY · GENERATIONS · TRAUMA

THE FOUNDATION
IDENTITY AND CULTURE
BIBLICAL TRUTH · ORIGINAL DESIGN

As you work your way toward freedom, notice these key elements in each chapter:

- **My Personal Stories.** Every chapter begins with my personal confessions to help you reflect on your own *heart wounds* that may still need mending. Your stories won't be just like mine, and that's okay. I encourage you to embrace *your* unique body image journey, while letting my stories serve as a guide.

- **Temple Truths.** Here we'll examine what God's Word has to say about the topic discussed in each chapter. While my experiences are personal, I back my opinions with scriptural truths and offer this book as a guide for a biblical body image movement.

- **Therapist Thoughts.** You'll find tips from therapists sprinkled throughout the book. Written in collaboration with my colleagues Dr. Linda Hoover, Dr. Mary Dainty, and Dr. Shannon Crawford, these will help you pause and reflect on the key takeaways in each chapter.

- **Body Image Blueprint.** At the end of each chapter, you'll find **a prayer, journal prompts, and activity/coloring sheets**. Please don't skip this section. When we rush past the processing, we don't create space for the Lord to do the deep work. Your real breakthrough will come as you make space for Him to speak directly to your heart and deepen your secure attachment to Him.

- **Strong Foundation Verses.** At the end of each chapter, you'll also find a list of scriptural truths relating to each specific topic. These verses will give you a strong foundation of truth to stand on when you need reminders about what God's Word has to say.

At the end of each unit, you'll find a **Counselor's Cornerstone** to help summarize the key takeaways. This section includes two parts:

1. **Strengthening Your Foundation:** a Bible study in which we'll explore what God's Word says about the unit's topic.
2. **Counselor's Chat:** an introduction to a video, in which I'll lead you through the **Therapy Toolbox** activities. You'll find the video link and the QR code on the next page. I suggest saving this link in your browser so you can easily access the videos.

I've written this book to be read from front to back; however, each chapter can also stand on its own. It's a good idea for you to keep this book tucked in your nightstand, as I anticipate that in the days, weeks, months, and even years to come, the Lord will ask you to revisit a specific chapter as He sheds new light on various body image issues.

Are you ready to partner with God to restore *your* body image? Then pull up a chair as I prayerfully walk you through this healing process. **Can I encourage you to invite a friend or family member to join you on this journey?** While I understand body image is sometimes a private thing, it's time to let others in so you can encourage and pray for one another along the way. Plus every journey is always more fun with friends!

Together, we go!

Access the Videos Here

https://davidccook.org/prd/restored

Access code: **RESTored**

Or scan this QR code:

Unit 1

The Foundation

Chapter 1

Choose a Building Site

The sweat dripped down my forehead as the lead instructor's face remained stoic. I'd taught group fitness for almost ten years, yet every new challenge had left me feeling vulnerable and unqualified. This particular training was structured as a weekend-long certification program followed by a video evaluation. My heart was racing while I waited for the examiner to announce whether I had passed the first part of the training. That day, about ten of us gathered in a small circle waiting for him to give feedback on the class I had just taught. Though we were standing in a large gymnasium, the room felt as though it were closing in around me.

"Rachael, you are one of the best instructors I have seen teach this format. You come alive when you get behind the microphone. But if you want to teach for our company, I need you to lose that mama pouch. Your son is almost three; what's your excuse for still having fat on your stomach?"

My heart still races when I think back to how that situation left me heartbroken. Essentially, I had the skills, but I couldn't play in his arena until I looked the part.

I went home from the training and cried, not just because the instructor had hurt my feelings but also because my mama pouch was one of my biggest insecurities. I had done everything I knew to eliminate it, yet it still clung stubbornly to my body. The lead instructor had voiced what I had been wrestling with in silence for years.

While what that man spoke into my life was hurtful, he was simply sharing what *he* knew to be true.

But it wasn't my truth.

The fitness-and-diet industry that shapes our culture does not have a biblical perspective. How could I hold a grudge against someone who was using a different guidebook than I was? We were simply speaking two different languages. While I can't be upset at the industry, I can be angry at the Enemy for wreaking havoc in this area of body image for far too long.

After that training, I told the Lord I could no longer teach group fitness. I was tired of all the striving and hustling. No matter how hard I tried, I never seemed to fit in with the fitness world.

A few weeks after I decided to quit teaching group fitness, I attended the Declare Conference for bloggers and speakers. At this conference, several vendors lined the halls. One particular booth caught my eye as I read the banner tagline, "Love God. Get Healthy. Be Whole. Love Others." I approached the booth to learn more, and the woman shared the vision behind the ministry, Revelation Wellness. Then she said, "Rachael, it's not about fitness. God loves you right where you are. Just show up." That woman's name was Alisa Keeton, and that day marks a moment on my body image timeline that God began the healing in my heart. I went on to become a Revelation Wellness instructor, and through that training, God started my restoration and rebuilding journey.

> No matter how hard I tried, I never seemed to fit in with the fitness world.

Did you notice the significant difference between these two encounters? One person told me I needed to lose my belly fat to participate, and the other told me to show up just as I am. Both shaped my core beliefs, but Alisa knew a secret the man did not yet know. She knew that God's perfect love casts out all fear (see 1 John 4:18).

Through Alisa and Revelation Wellness, God helped me lay a new, solid foundation on His truth, and I want that same freedom for you.

Therapist Thoughts

Core beliefs are an individual's central ideas about herself, others, and the world. These beliefs act like a lens through which every situation is seen, and they shape how a person sees the world. Harmful core beliefs lead to negative thoughts, feelings, and behaviors, whereas rational core beliefs lead to positive reactions.

Temple Truths

When the fitness "expert" told me what he believed to be true about my body, I believed his distorted view of truth. But now that I've healed, I compare his words to an old, out-of-date structure that needed to be demolished. To build a sound body image, we must first tear down the old beliefs that no longer apply. This idea is based on Psalm 127:1, which says, "Unless the LORD builds the house, those who build it labor in vain" (ESV). In other words, if we want a solid foundation on which to stand, we must uproot all the principles we've held about our bodies that are not given to us from God.

Jesus' words in Matthew 7:24–27 give us a beautiful picture of why it is crucial to build on a solid foundation:

> Everyone then who hears these words of mine and does them will be like a wise man who built his house on the rock. And the rain fell, and the floods came, and the winds blew and beat on that house, but it did not fall, because it had been founded on the rock. And everyone who hears these words of mine and does not do them will be like a foolish man who built his house on the sand. And the rain fell, and the floods came, and the winds blew and beat against that house, and it fell, and great was the fall of it. (ESV)

My father is a retired general contractor, and I learned a lot about construction by going with him to different job sites. I remember one piece of lakefront property a customer wanted to purchase. After Dad inspected the property along with other experts in the field, the property was deemed unsafe for constructing a house.

This was heartbreaking news because the property offered a beautiful lakefront view and appeared to be the perfect spot for this family. From the outside looking in, this piece of land had it all. But if this family had chosen to throw caution to the wind and build in that location, their home would not have withstood the test of time.

Likewise, when our body image is built on faulty foundational beliefs, we'll lack the spiritual stability needed to weather life's storms.

> To stop ourselves from sinking, we must take the time to build our body image on a spiritual foundation of solid rock.

What do the storms of body image look like? Well, they come in many forms, including weight gain, weight loss, illness, expectations, comparison, and idle words, to name a few.

Notice how the passage we just read from Matthew tells us *when* the rain and the winds come, not *if* they come. I can't keep those storms from coming your way, but I can give you tools to help you feel prepared when they do arrive. To stop ourselves from sinking, we must take the time to build our body image on a spiritual foundation of solid rock.

Don't just take my word for it. The Bible makes it clear that we should build on the solid foundation of Christ:

- Mark 12:10 reminds us that Jesus was the stone that the builders rejected and that He is now our cornerstone.
- Ephesians 2:20–21 says that together we are His house, built on the foundation of the apostles and the prophets. The passage emphasizes that

the cornerstone is Christ Jesus Himself and that we are carefully joined together in Him, becoming a holy temple for the Lord.

- According to 1 Corinthians 3:10, because of God's grace, we can lay the foundation like expert builders with hopes that others will build on it.

As you begin this body image journey, know that you are building a solid foundation not only for you to stand on but for future generations to build on. This new way of viewing body image changes the trajectory of your family lineage, and I consider that to be a cause worth fighting for.

Building on the rock is as simple as letting Jesus, our cornerstone, into this body image journey. Let's start by debunking common cultural messages about our bodies and by choosing instead to stand firmly on the Word of God.

As you review the following chart, consider the contrast between cultural lies and God's truth.

Cultural Lie versus Truth from God's Word	
Lie: My weight is my worth.	**Truth:** Jesus paid it all. My worth is in Him. (1 Cor. 6:20)
Lie: There's something wrong with my body.	**Truth:** My body is God's own temple, and it is sacred. (1 Cor. 3:17; 6:19)
Lie: I need to hustle to keep up with the world's beauty standards so I can fulfill my call.	**Truth:** God has already laid the plans for my life. No need to hustle to make them come to pass. (Eph. 2:10)
Lie: Outward beauty is worth more than inner beauty.	**Truth:** God values my unfading beauty. (1 Pet. 3:3–4)

The list of lies could go on for pages. However, another problem we often encounter is that some of these lies are so deeply ingrained that we don't even recognize them as false anymore. In the body image blueprint exercise, you will get a chance to fill in your own lies that need to be replaced with God's truth. But first, let's identify how to spot a deeply embedded cultural lie.

These tips will help you become aware of any areas of your body image not built on the solid foundation of God's Word:

- Is this belief or behavior life-giving? Or does it suck the life out of you? If something is draining you, then chances are it's founded on sinking sand.
- Have you spoken this belief out loud to someone else? When we bring things into the light, we expose anything that is not from the Lord.
- How is your self-talk? Culture has normalized talking poorly about our bodies. It's not okay, and it stops with us today.

This process of establishing a solid foundation will take time and practice. Start by standing on one verse at a time and letting Jesus plant your feet firmly on the truth He offers you.

Body Image Blueprint

Now it's time to pray, process, and praise through what we just learned.

Let's Pray

Jesus, I invite You on this journey to restore my body image. I can't do this without You. You are the only rock I want to stand on. I release control to You. Amen.

Use the space provided to write your own prayer.

Pause to Process

1. Write about a time you felt you were sinking.

_____

_____

_____

_____

_____

_____

_____

_____

_____

_____

2. During that season, in what ways were you standing on the solid rock of biblical truth? In what ways were you standing on the sinking sand of cultural lies?

_____

_____

_____

_____

_____

_____

_____

_____

_____

_____

_____

_____

_____

_____

_____

_____

Now it's your turn to challenge a cultural lie. Fill in the blank spaces with any cultural lies you've been wrestling with regarding your body image. Replace those lies with scriptural truths.

Lie: (List a cultural lie you wrestle with.)

Truth: (List a truth you've found in God's Word.)

Strong Foundation Verses

Use the following scriptural truths to strengthen your foundation. Consider saying them aloud, taking a picture of them to reference, or writing one that stands out on a sticky note and putting it where you will see it daily.

- Jesus is the foundation. (1 Cor. 3:10–11)
- Anyone who hears God's words and puts them into action is like a wise man who built his house on the rock. (Matt. 7:24–27)
- The people gave a shout of praise because the foundation of the Lord was laid. (Ezra 3:11)
- In the beginning, God laid the foundations of the earth. (Ps. 102:25)
- "He will be the sure foundation for your times." (Isa. 33:6)
- "God's solid foundation stands firm." (2 Tim. 2:19)

Let's Rest in God's Word

Coloring is a therapeutic tool used by many counselors, yet many of us don't give ourselves space for this simple but powerful activity.[1] How cool that our Creator gave us many creative outlets to process our thoughts and emotions! Throughout the book, meditate on the key verse as you color, and thank God for your body—exactly as it is today.

PUT THEM INTO

PRACTICE

THEREFORE EVERYONE WHO HEARS THESE WORDS OF MINE
AND PUTS THEM INTO PRACTICE IS LIKE A WISE MAN
WHO BUILT HIS HOUSE ON THE ROCK.
MATTHEW 7:24

Chapter 2

Cracks in the Foundation

Before you get too impressed by the fact that I taught group fitness for more than a decade, let's back up to where it all began. As a kid and early teenager, I would have been voted the least likely to grow up and teach exercise classes. I moved at such a snail's pace during one middle school track practice that by the time I returned from our three-mile run, everyone, including my coach, had packed up and gone home. My coaches couldn't wrap their brains around how someone could move so slowly. Deep down, I knew they thought I was being lazy, but in reality, I was running as fast as my short legs could carry me.

At school, the only boys who ever talked to me were the ones who wanted me to ask my friends out for them. To be honest, it didn't bother me all that much. That is, until I tasted what it was like to get some attention.

In high school, I played basketball. As with my track experience, the term *played* meant I warmed the bench and cheered on my teammates. The only time I saw the court was if we were double-digit points ahead with one minute left in the game. When the coach would finally put me in, the crowd would erupt in cheers as they hoped and prayed I could make a basket.

My basketball career came to a screeching halt when I developed a hip abnormality that caused my growth plates to grow apart rather than together. The pain became so unbearable that I couldn't walk upstairs without crying. At the time, the only thing the doctor knew to do was tell me to rest. So I hung up my bench-warming jersey and stopped practicing with the team. But before I left the doctor's office, he gave me a final word of advice: "Rachael, it wouldn't hurt if you lost some weight."

While it was good advice related to a hip problem, it did not come with any how-tos. I had already been practicing with the track team and the basketball team. I didn't know how to control my weight at that age.

Desperate to feel better, I decided to give up soda and candy bars. Would you believe I lost about thirty pounds within a month? It was the first and *only* time in my life that weight "fell off." And the pounds just kept dropping.

Not long after my sudden weight loss, my family and I took a vacation to Florida, where I got a nice tan and bleach-blonde highlights—quite a change for this dark brunette. When I returned to school the following week, I received lots of looks as I walked down the hall. For the first time in my life, boys noticed me. Not only did they see me, but they also wanted to talk to me. Just like that, I had gone from being unseen to being seen. And with that, I transitioned from feeling unloved to loved.

On my body image timeline, this pivotal moment marks the point when obsession began. I tried every diet technique. I overexercised. And I eventually pursued a career in health and exercise science, determined to learn everything I could about the human body.

In hindsight, I recognize that this season twisted my true identity. At first, the weight loss was good for my health. But in time, it turned unhealthy as obsessive behaviors entered my life. Giving up soda and candy bars is a smart choice for anyone, as neither of those provides nutrient-rich fuel for our bodies. But the Enemy specializes in taking something good and adding a plot twist. In this incident, he reduced my identity and worth solely to the appearance of my body.

If you take away only one principle from this story, please remember this: Our body image battle is more profound than what we can see. It is spiritual warfare.

Therapist Thoughts

Have you ever considered how the original sin involved food? Unlike other addictions, food cannot simply be avoided—not if we hope to live! What a vicious hijack by the Enemy to take something God intended to be a blessing and turn it into a source of struggle and shame. (Dr. Linda Hoover)

When my self-worth deviated from the foundation of who God created me to be, I became me-focused rather than kingdom-focused. The Enemy would like us to become so obsessed with looking down at our bodies that we forget to look up at Jesus.

This is the part of the story where the tug-of-war begins.

On the one hand, taking care of our bodies through proper nutrition and movement is important. The human body is comprised of joints, tendons, ligaments, muscles, and many other pieces that help us move. For example, I can see my fingers moving with incredible speed and accuracy as I type this manuscript. I am not telling my fingers to move; instead, signals are coming from my brain to my nerves, which, in turn, let the muscles know it's time to get moving.

> The Enemy would like us to become so obsessed with looking down at our bodies that we forget to look up at Jesus.

When Matt and I were engaged, we took Human Gross Anatomy together (no, I'm not saying it was gross; that was the name of the course). Our love bloomed as we worked together as exercise physiology majors to dissect human cadavers that had been donated for scientific research. Romantic, I know.

Matt went on to take five more anatomy labs for his doctoral degree, but thankfully, I only had to take that one course. During that time, our class dissected ten cadavers in total. I was surprised to discover that none of them looked the same on the inside. Not only were they different in size, shape, and construction, but one of the cadavers was missing its latissimus dorsi muscles (the large muscles of the back). Isn't that crazy? If I learned anything from that class, it's that no two of us are the same externally or internally, which means our bodies cannot all follow the same formula to look or perform the same way.

One thing that is the same, however, is that God created our bodies to move, and He gave us whole foods to keep us moving well.

By design, fueling our bodies with whole foods and balanced nutrition is instinctual. We certainly weren't born craving candy bars and soda. But somewhere along the way, our culture created unhealthy beliefs and behaviors, leading many of us to swing to extremes when it comes to diet and exercise. The Enemy has no new tricks up his sleeve. The best he can do is twist what God meant for good. This means we must be careful not to take the bait and slip into an obsession with food, exercise, and unhealthy body image ideals.

When it comes to diet fads and exercise programs, believe me when I say I have been there, done that. In fact, I have every size shirt to prove it. These moments create a faulty foundation in our body image house, often resulting in idols that wreak havoc in our hearts.

Temple Truths

Before we go much further, it's time to discuss why I named the Bible teachings throughout the book "Temple Truths." This word *temple* has been thrown around a lot in the Christian culture. If you're like me, you might roll your eyes upon hearing it, as it has often been misused as an excuse to obsess over our bodies. This confusion about the temple creates a significant crack in our body image foundation.

In chapter 1, we discussed why it's essential to build our identity on the solid rock of God's truth rather than the sinking sand of cultural lies. But even the strongest structures can suffer damage from life's storms. That's why it's important to repair any cracks that may form in our foundation.

I'm no expert builder, so I sought the advice of my father (the contractor), who has built many homes. Here's what I learned from him about cracks in a foundation:

> If the foundation collapses, the house collapses. I don't mean it necessarily falls by collapse, but it's damaged and doesn't look right or function properly. One unmitigated issue leads to another. Cracks can be caused by heaving or buckling in the soil, frequently caused by extreme cold and thawing.

The parallels are many when the foundation of our body image is faulty. Due to cultural messages that bring us through emotional extremes, we develop cracks in our foundation.

While we may not notice them at first, they can make their way into our hearts, causing permanent damage that threatens to take us down spiritually, emotionally, psychologically, and physically.

As a science girl with a counselor's mind, I often ask the question, "Why?" But as a counselor, I've been taught not to ask my clients why because it elicits a defense mechanism in most people. I don't hesitate to bring my curiosities to God, though. I know He can handle my tough questions. So, years ago, when I began to ask Him *why* we have this body image battle, He directed me to study the temple.

According to the Blue Letter Bible, the temple is referenced 683 times in the NIV translation of the Bible. Anytime God mentions a concept this frequently, it's probably a good idea for us to pay close attention. (To be clear, if God mentions something even once, it matters. But the math nerd in me got pretty excited to see Him bring up the temple so many times!)

Biblical Greek offers two words for "temple": *naos* and *hieron. Hieron* would designate the outer court and the temple proper, whereas *naos* refers to the inner sanctuary of the temple known as the Most Holy Place or the Holy of Holies. This is the place where the ark of the Lord resided.

If you're like me and need to see something to understand it, check out this visual illustration of the temple:

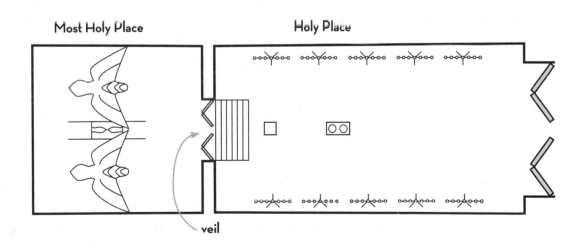

Most Holy Place　　　　　　**Holy Place**

veil

A thick, heavy curtain, or veil, separated the Most Holy Place—which housed the Spirit of God—from the Holy Place. Only once a year was a high priest allowed to enter the Most Holy Place to offer a blood sacrifice. This is significant because of what our great high priest, Jesus, did on the cross: "At that moment the curtain of the temple was torn in two from top to bottom. The earth shook, the rocks split" (Matt. 27:51).

When the curtain tore in the temple as Jesus died on the cross, this was a representation of the shift that took place in the supernatural realm. With the death of Christ, we were given access to the presence of God. In this moment, the temple became more than just a physical building—our living, breathing bodies became God's temples!

We house the Spirit of God everywhere we go.

In fact, the word *naos*, indicating the holiest place, is used in Paul's teachings six times when referring to the body as the temple. We see this term used in reference to both an individual body and the church body.

For the individual: "Didn't you realize that your body is a sacred place, the place of the Holy Spirit? Don't you see that you can't live however you please, squandering what God paid such a high price for? The physical part of you is not some piece of property belonging to the spiritual part of you. God owns the whole works. So let people see God in and through your body" (1 Cor. 6:19–20 MSG).

For the church: "Don't you realize that all of you together are the temple of God and that the Spirit of God lives in you? God will destroy anyone who destroys this temple. For God's temple is holy, and you are that temple" (1 Cor. 3:16–17 NLT).

God's Word tells us that we are mobile temples. We house the Spirit of God everywhere we go.

This, my friends, is why the Enemy's attack on our bodies is so strong.

Because we are Christians, this should not bring fear; instead, it brings hope because we know exactly what is needed to fight this battle. This battle cannot be won with weapons of weight loss, perfection, or a new gadget that makes us promises it can't keep. We win this body image battle by putting on the full armor of God: the belt of truth buckled around our waists, the breastplate of righteousness in place, our feet fitted with the readiness that comes from the gospel of peace, the shield of faith, the helmet of salvation, and the sword of the Spirit (see Eph. 6:10–18).

Put on your armor, my friends. This is war.

Body Image Blueprint

Now it's time to pray, process, and praise through what we just learned.

Let's Pray

God, thank You that You sent Jesus, Your only Son, to die on the cross that I might be united with You. Thank You for living in me. Help me honor my temple in a way that brings glory to You. I am suiting up for battle with my armor in place. In Jesus' name, amen.

Use the space provided to write your own prayer.

Pause to Process

1. Write about your body image battle and the belief that your body is a temple.

_____

_____

_____

_____

_____

_____

_____

_____

2. Is this a new concept for you?

    A. If yes, what came up when you read this chapter?

    B. If no, what is something new God is showing you about how He views your temple?

    (We'll use these answers in this section's Counselor's Cornerstone activity.)

_____

_____

_____

_____

_____

_____

Strong Foundation Verses

Use the following scriptural truths to strengthen your foundation. Consider saying them aloud, taking a picture of them to reference, or writing one that stands out on a sticky note and putting it somewhere you will see it daily.

- In the New Testament, the word *temple* describes Christ's human body. (John 2:19–21)
- Believers are called the temple of God. (1 Cor. 3:16–17)
- The church is described as "a holy temple in the Lord." (Eph. 2:21–22)
- Scripture offers a simple prayer to seek the Lord in His holy temple. (Ps. 27:4)
- The Bible gives us a way to meditate on His unfailing love. (Ps. 48:9)

Let's Rest in God's Word

As you complete this chapter's therapeutic coloring activity, meditate on the key verse and thank God for your body—exactly as it is today.

DON'T YOU KNOW THAT YOU YOURSELVES ARE GOD'S TEMPLE AND THAT GOD'S SPIRIT DWELLS IN YOUR MIDST?

1 CORINTHIANS 3:16

Chapter 3

The Original Design

Are you kind to your body? I learned the importance of body kindness the hard way when Matt and I trained for a rim-to-rim hike of the Grand Canyon with Revelation Wellness.

It started as a worthy mission to hike 23.9 treacherous miles across the Grand Canyon in a single day. That's almost the length of a marathon—while tackling some of the steepest, most challenging trails in the nation.

Every year, Revelation Wellness takes a group of men and women on this journey through the canyon, and it promised to be unlike anything we'd ever experienced. To join, each individual commits to raising a set amount of money for the nonprofit ministry and to fully completing the training program months in advance.

The training program wasn't about burning calories or getting bikini-body ready. Instead, it was designed to prepare us for the endurance necessary to complete the trek safely. Because we were from Texas, everyone referred to us as "the flatlanders." We would hike for miles but only get hundreds of feet of elevation gain when the goal was to reach thousands. Concerned, our team leaders informed us that if we couldn't show 4,000 feet of gains in our final training hike, then we couldn't go on the trip.

At first, we considered flying to a location with mountain trails. But as the parents of three young kids, we knew that wasn't an option. Determined to complete this challenge, we went to the tallest hill we could find near us in Texas. That hill had a one-hundred-foot incline, so we set out to do forty-six hill repeats in hopes of totaling four thousand feet.

If only there had been an elevator right next to that hill that could take us down so we could hike back up, those hill repeats would have been manageable. But because we had to go up and back down so many times, it took seven and a half hours and sixteen miles to complete the requirements. We were exhausted and sore, but the real thing that got my attention the next day was the twinge at the back of my heel into my ankle. While those hill repeats had helped us reach our training requirements, the repetitive motion had caused me to develop Achilles tendinitis.

If you've ever experienced a stress injury like Achilles tendinitis or plantar fasciitis, you probably cringed when you read that last line. That suffix *-itis* at the end of a medical term simply means "inflammation of" whatever root word it is attached to. Inflammation is our bodies' way of saying to us, *Please, stop what you're doing and take care of me.* Unfortunately, we don't always listen when our bodies speak, and if we continue to push onward, we only make the inflammation worse.

That's exactly what happened when I went hiking in the canyon. The pain during the first half of the canyon became excruciating as we tackled the steep descent in the early morning hours. It shot through my foot, ankle, and leg with each step I took. As we reached the half-way point, I leaned over to my husband and asked him to pray for me. I wasn't sure I could make it the rest of the way, but after we stopped to pray, the pain completely vanished for the remainder of the hike. Much to my surprise, I walked out of the canyon pain-free! This shift in pain also resulted in a shift in my perspective of that journey. My prayers went from "Dear God, please help me survive this day" to "Wow, Lord! Your creation all around me in this canyon is breathtaking!"

Therapist Thoughts

Learn to listen to the messages your body sends through both pain and pleasure. Make a list of things that feel kind to your body, and implement them in your self-care routine.

I wish the story ended there. But when we returned home from our hike, the pain became intense once again. I wasn't mad at God, but I was angry at my body. No one else had developed Achilles tendinitis on that hike. Why had I? I felt powerless, frustrated, and confused.

I will not bore you with my two-year journey of recovery from that stress-induced injury, but I do want to share the powerful life lessons I learned along the way.

Four Lessons We Can Learn about Our Bodies from an Injury

1. *God is never the source of our pain.* It's dangerous territory to assume God sends illness and injury our way to teach us lessons. While He does not send these trials, He is present and ready to redeem what the Enemy meant for evil.

2. *Your body is not the enemy.* While I was mad at my body, it was not her fault. She responded the best she could in telling me that something was off. She knew if I didn't start resting with intention, the stress injury would be the least of my concerns. Your body is *for* you. Listen to her.

3. *Weakness reveals our underlying fear.* When my body doesn't respond the way I want it to, I feel weak and out of control. When I am sick or injured, I feel helpless. This injury revealed that my hope and trust had rested in my ability to be strong. This works when we operate in our strengths, which is a futile goal. In our weaknesses, we are forced to come toe to toe with the reality that we have limitations. For this reason, weaknesses are a gift. In our weaknesses, God's power is revealed to the fullest, and we learn that we must rely on His strengths.

4. *Our original design was to be with and rest in God.* When we operate from a place of hustle, inflammation takes over our hearts and wreaks havoc in our bodies.

Temple Truths

When contractors build a home, they refer to the original blueprints. If they only looked at the plan once and attempted to build the home from memory, the finished house would probably not look like or function according to its original design. To go back to the original design of the human body, we must ask God for His plan in our being and doing, and that starts by restoring union with Him.

When looking at our blueprint, the Bible, we start with Adam and Eve, since they were the first humans God created to be in relationship with Him. Most remember Eve by what she did wrong, but have you ever stopped to imagine her life before the fall? I love daydreaming about what life must have been for these lovebirds.

The Bible describes a garden full of trees that were pleasant to look at and good sources of food. Yes, there was a time when people ate their fruits and vegetables not because they had to; rather, it was all their taste buds knew, and they liked it! As Adam and Eve strolled through this garden, they didn't recognize they were naked because their focus wasn't yet on themselves. There was no disconnect between their bodies, souls, minds, and spirits because they were in perfect union with God. Adam and Eve walked together with God as they enjoyed the beauty of Eden. They felt nothing but joy, peace, and love. Life in the garden was perfect! Until … until a crack came and destroyed their firm foundation.

The verse we read about Adam and Eve *before* the fall seems too good to be true: "Adam and his wife were both naked, and they felt no shame" (Gen. 2:25).

Go back and read that again, if it didn't hit you the first time.

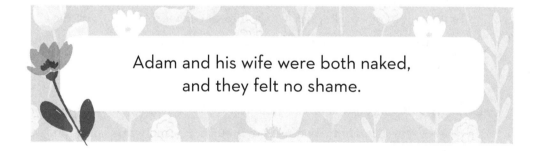

Adam and his wife were both naked,
and they felt no shame.

Adam and Eve walked, talked, and shared life with each other and God while they were completely naked—and *they felt no shame*. I have a tough time walking naked from the shower to my closet without feeling shame. But to walk in a garden with another person without the urge to cover up is mind-blowing. This naked freedom was short-lived for the happy couple, as we see in Genesis 3:7–9:

Then the eyes of both of them were opened, and they *realized* they were naked; so they sewed fig leaves together and made *coverings* for themselves.

Then the man and his wife heard the sound of the LORD God as he was walking in the garden in the cool of the day, and they *hid* from the LORD God among the trees of the garden. But the LORD God called to the man, "Where are you?"

In chapter 2, we discussed cracks in the foundation, and how they can bring our entire house, or temple, down. The verses we just read in Genesis 3 show the first crack in the foundation of man's union with God. Within moments of the crack that ushered in sin to the world, we watch Adam and Eve take three actions:

1. They *realized* they were naked.
2. They *covered* their bodies in shame.
3. They *hid* from God.

Their new realization came from knowledge that God never intended for them. Aware that their naked glory was over, they *covered* themselves with a false sense of security. Then they *hid* from the Lord.

My friend, many of us are making the same shame-filled decisions over our bodies today. We have a hyperawareness of our bodies that was never God's original design. We hide behind false coverings of pride, shame, lust, and excessive pursuit of our skewed body image goals. But perhaps the most heartbreaking of all actions is our hiding from God. As believers, we know the love of God, yet we often choose to walk this body image road without Him. It's almost as though we viewed God as the old parent who isn't with the times, when He's the only one we should be running to, to restore our original design.

Even though Adam and Eve hid from God, He *immediately* came looking for them. In His infinite mercy and grace, He continues to come looking for us when we try to hide. We see God pursue this restoration in 2 Corinthians 6:16: "I will live with them and walk among them, and I will be their God, and they will be my people."

We see God longing to walk with us again. It's a picture of the complete restoration of our original design. God's original design for our bodies is that we walk, talk, and live in union with Him. He is our God, and we are His people. That, my friends, is the most comforting news. This need to strive for perfection in order to show up for God is gone.

I recognize that we live in a fallen world that makes it challenging to rest in this truth. If we didn't, we could stop this book right here. But before we move into the following chapters, please rest in the fact that God is pursuing a relationship with you right where you are in your body. Right now.

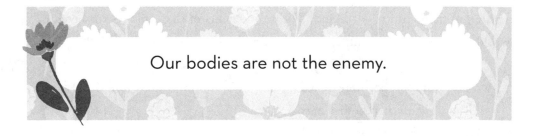

Our bodies are not the enemy.

But just as I grew frustrated with my body when injuries kept me in pain, I've yet to meet a woman who has never faced a moment in life when she felt her body had let her down.

Why is it that we have an easy time receiving God's grace in our spirits but when it comes to our bodies … we are often at war? Perhaps we need to step back and remember that our bodies are not the enemy.

Your body is a gift from God.

Let me say that again. Your body is a gift from God.

Body Image Blueprint

Now it's time to pray, process, and praise through what we just learned.

Let's Pray

God, I want to walk and talk with You on this body image journey. Thank You for always coming to find me when I hide. I open my heart to You today. I trust You. Please forgive me for rejecting my body. I want to restore union with You and my body. In Jesus' name, amen.

Use the space provided to write your own prayer.

Pause to Process

1. What is your relationship with your body? Would you call her a distant acquaintance, an enemy, or your best friend?

_____

_____

_____

_____

_____

_____

2. It's time for a ceasefire in the war against our bodies. Use the space provided to write a love letter to your body and an apology for how you've treated or spoken to her.

_____

_____

_____

_____

_____

_____

_____

_____

_____

_____

Strong Foundation Verses

Use the following scriptural truths to strengthen your foundation. Consider saying them aloud, taking a picture of them to reference, or writing one that stands out on a sticky note and putting it somewhere you will see it daily.

- In union with Christ you have been brought to fullness. (Col. 2:10)
- The Father protects you by the power of His name. (John 17:11)
- The Holy Spirit is your advocate, who will teach you all things. (John 14:26)
- Christ gave the apostles, prophets, evangelists, pastors, and teachers so the body of Christ may be built up and reach unity in the faith. (Eph. 4:11–13)
- Love binds all virtues together in perfect unity. (Col. 3:14)

Let's Rest in God's Word

As you complete this chapter's therapeutic coloring activity, meditate on the key verse and thank God for your body—exactly as it is today.

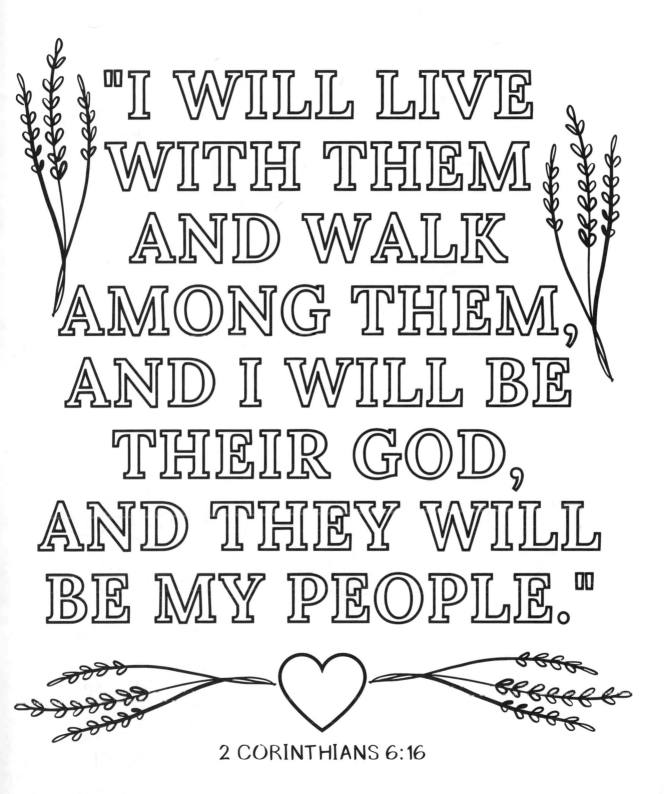

"I WILL LIVE WITH THEM AND WALK AMONG THEM, AND I WILL BE THEIR GOD, AND THEY WILL BE MY PEOPLE."

2 CORINTHIANS 6:16

Unit 1 Counselor's Cornerstone

Strengthening Your Foundation

As we discussed in chapter 2, the Bible has a lot to say about the temple throughout the Old and New Testaments. Let's take a deep dive into the "then" and "now" elements of a few of the temple areas so we can see how they relate to Jesus.

1. **Brazen Altar:** *Then*, God required a sacrifice of a perfect animal. *Now*, Jesus is our perfect sacrifice. Read Leviticus 17:11; John 1:29; Hebrews 9:25; and Revelation 13:8. What did you notice?

_____

_____

2. **Holy Place:** *Then*, only priests could enter. *Now*, believers in Jesus have been made holy through Jesus and can go directly to God. Read Hebrews 9–10. Write one thing the Lord showed you.

_____

_____

3. **Veil:** *Then*, the veil, or curtain, as the New International Version renders it, separated the Holy Place from the Most Holy Place. Only once a year could priests enter. When Jesus died on the cross, the temple veil tore in two from top to bottom. *Now*, believers can enter God's presence directly at any time. Read Exodus 26; 2 Chronicles 3:14; Matthew 27:51; and Hebrews 10:19–22. What did you notice?

_____

_____

4. **Most Holy Place:** *Then,* this was God's throne room, where He would meet and give His commands. *Now,* believers in Jesus can come boldly before God's throne of grace. Read Hebrews 4:16. Have you ever entered God's throne room boldly to ask for healing in your body and restoration in your body image?

Counselor's Chat

In the unit 1 video, I'm speaking life over your foundation and your union with the Lord. I will walk you through the following counseling activity and speak a blessing of union over your body. You can access the video with the QR code on page 22.

Therapy Toolbox

In this unit, we've talked about building on a solid foundation, watching for cracks in that foundation, and restoring union with God and your body. Using the Restored Body House, let's chart where you are today at the beginning of our body image journey. (You will get a chance at the end of the book to revisit a similar image to celebrate your progress.)

Use the following prompts to fill in The Restored Body House:

- What foundation are you standing on? Is your temple built on the solid rock foundation of God's truth? Or are you standing on the shifting sands of cultural lies? On the lines provided, write specific beliefs you are currently standing on, both good and bad. Then circle or highlight anything you want to keep standing on, and cross out anything that needs to be removed from your foundation.
- Next, write what you want to lay at the feet of Jesus in relation to your body image. Write things such as disappointments, expectations, fears, doubts, losses, or anything else the Lord brings to mind.
- As you color the doodles outside the house, ask the Lord to restore union with Him and with your body. It's hard to follow the directions of the builder if you don't trust where He is leading you.

THE RESTORED BODY HOUSE

PSALM 127:1

UNLESS THE LORD BUILDS THE
HOUSE, ITS BUILDERS LABOR IN VAIN

WHAT I'M LAYING DOWN

WHAT I'M STANDING ON

UNIT 1

Unit 2

The Floor Plan

Chapter 4

Structural Stories

Picture me as a young girl. Still in shock that a Gulf Coast Florida beach town would be my new home for the year, I took slow steps across the bridge to my new middle school, admiring the beautiful palm trees. With that wonder and excitement also came debilitating fear: *What will they think of me? Will I make any friends? Is this sweater vest the right outfit choice?*

Can we take a moment of silence for the sweater vest craze? Perhaps it was just a small-town fashion trend, but that particular day I was rocking a cobalt blue sweater vest with a lime green stripe directly across my chest. Thank you very much.

The thoughts of my sweater vest quickly dissipated as I rounded the corner and found myself alone in a sea of middle schoolers. I promptly chose my seat and did my best to focus on class. As the bell rang for lunch, I got in line with the rest of the group, though I was the only one who didn't have a friend to sit with in the cafeteria.

My palms began to sweat as I grabbed my tan, slightly damp tray and made my way through the line. Much to my surprise, a tall, handsome boy asked my name and invited me to sit at his table. Although joining a group of boys was not at the top of my list, I was thrilled to have an invite, so I said yes. The lunchroom was serving chicken-fried steak, though I question if that's indeed what it was, and I couldn't wait to dig into it with my soon-to-be new friends.

But then, while on my way to the handsome boy's table, he laughed and made a statement I will never forget: "HA! You didn't think I was serious, did you, chubby? Only hot girls can sit with us."

I swallowed hard, held back my tears, and managed to say, "Of course not." Then I found a table across the room, where I sat alone.

My appetite was gone, and I spent the next half hour dabbing my chicken-fried whatever into my potatoes. I was so mortified by this event that I didn't even tell my family what had happened. When asked about my first day of school, I plastered on a fake smile and said what every parent wants to hear: "It was good."

While eighth-grade Rachael tried to sweep that humiliating episode under the rug and pretend it never happened, it turned out to be a defining moment that would shape what I believed about myself, others, and my body for many years to come.

Here are just a few of the lies the Enemy deposited into my heart in that one moment:

- *If you weren't so fat, those boys would have let you stay.*
- *Food is your only friend.*
- *You will always be alone.*
- *You have to earn your worth.*
- *You do not deserve a seat at the table.*

That last lie has debilitated me throughout my adult life. As I've counseled women, I've noticed I am not alone in believing there is no room at the table unless I earn it. The quest for the perfect body is one of the many ways we are tempted to earn our worth. As you will find out in chapters to come, that lie impacted my identity for years.

When I discovered I could control my weight and outward appearance, it gave me a false sense of control. I came to believe that I could earn a seat at any table as long as I looked the part. And, to be honest, losing weight did earn me a seat at many tables, albeit the wrong ones. At the root of this lie was a young girl's longing for identity and belonging.

These defining moments in our lives can establish our core beliefs about ourselves and our place in the world. In this section, we will begin the fun process of writing your **body image timeline**. I call it "fun" because this is where freedom begins. The purpose of our timelines isn't to blame people for our struggles but to pinpoint lies the Enemy has planted in our hearts—lies that need to be uprooted.

In unit 1, we built a solid foundation of faith to stand upon. Now we get to unpack beliefs and moments the Enemy would love for us never to think or talk about. We get to bring secrets up and out of our hearts that have been lodged there for too long. In doing so, you will get the opportunity to fill in the blanks with your personal stories. But before we do that, let's look at stories that shaped a few women of the Bible.

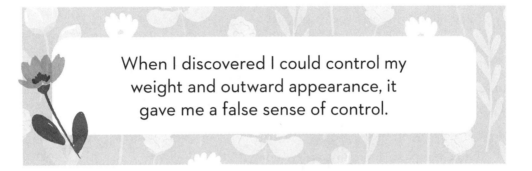

When I discovered I could control my weight and outward appearance, it gave me a false sense of control.

Temple Truths

Years ago, when Matt and I were looking to purchase our first home, our real estate agent took us on a home tour adventure. We saw so many homes in one day that they all became a big blur. The agent would share many facts about each home, listing the number of bedrooms, the year it had been built, and other details most homeowners would want to know. But what I remember the most were the stories. Sometimes the stories were sweet, like the one about a new baby that one couple had brought home. But others repelled us from buying, like the story involving a room dedicated to satanic worship rituals. We weren't allowed to see that room because it was considered sacred to the owners. Needless to say, we passed on that home. Yet any time I drive by that neighborhood, I still think of that home's story.

Throughout the Bible, we see many of these "structural" stories shaping people for good. Like when David defeated Goliath ... I'm sure David would say that this defining moment boosted his confidence in himself and, more importantly, solidified his faith in God.

As a counselor, I'm always looking for the untold story. I like to read between the lines and see what isn't said. It is there that we find the real story. Let's use this approach for a moment to examine the defining moments of two women in the Bible.

We will begin with Eve. We know that she felt shame and hid after disobeying God (see Gen. 3:7). Have you ever looked at the last words God spoke to her in the Bible?

> I will make your pains in childbearing very severe;
>   with painful labor you will give birth to children.
> Your desire will be for your husband,
>   and he will rule over you. (Gen. 3:16)

We know that God had already put a plan in motion to send Jesus to redeem Eve and future generations. Jesus would be the One who would carry this weight that was placed on Eve, as we read in Isaiah 53:5:

> But he was pierced for our transgressions,
>   he was crushed for our iniquities;
> the punishment that brought us peace was on him,
>   and by his wounds we are healed.

We know this truth because we have lived long enough to see the redemption piece of the story. But Eve did not know this yet. Oh, what I would give to read Eve's journal after God explained the consequences of her actions. I imagine it might say something like this: *"Dear Diary, I really blew it this time. I ate from the one tree we were ordered to stay away from. Somehow I found myself biting into that juicy apple. What was I thinking? Now we have to leave our home, and I will have painful labor, whatever that even means. I would give anything to go back and make a different choice."*

Therapist Thoughts

Journaling is a great way to process emotions and events. This practice can also be used to help you notice themes in your life. If you find it hard to write long journal entries, try using bullet points instead.

The Bible doesn't say what Eve believed about herself after the fall, but I imagine she gave herself a mental beating. When she received this consequence of her sin, she didn't have a therapist to process it with or even another woman to share in her pain. She must have felt alone, afraid, and unworthy.

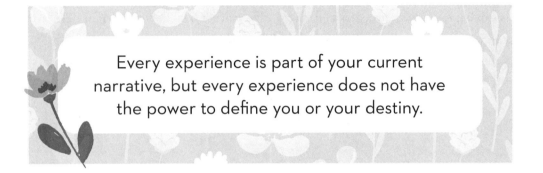

Every experience is part of your current narrative, but every experience does not have the power to define you or your destiny.

Next, let's look at Mary, the mother of Jesus. Unlike Eve, Mary had done nothing wrong. Matthew 1:18 tells us, "His mother Mary was pledged to be married to Joseph, but before they came together, she was found to be pregnant through the Holy Spirit."

Mary's diary is another one I would love to get my hands on. (Yes, I realize these women did not have diaries, but dream with me as we explore their thoughts.) In my opinion, it would read something like this: *"Dear Diary, I'm pregnant! I haven't even known a man, but I am pregnant! Who is going to believe that it was the Holy Spirit who came upon me?"*

And as her belly grew, her diary might have transitioned to: *"Dear Diary, I can feel the stares from the other women as I walk through town. I can hear them whisper behind my back. They act as though I don't exist when I enter the room. I feel alone and afraid. Dear God, please help me be strong."*

What do *you* think Eve and Mary might have believed about themselves after these defining moments shaped the trajectory of their lives?

While Eve did sin, God quickly set a plan in motion to redeem what she had lost. Ephesians 1:7 says "In him [Jesus] we have redemption through his blood, the forgiveness of sins, in accordance with the riches of God's grace." It was by the grace of God that He sent Jesus, who shed His blood for any moments in our stories for which we need forgiveness!

On the other hand, Mary did not sin in her story, yet this defining moment still had to be the hardest thing she had ever endured in her life. Mary's willingness to carry and protect the Savior of the world helped bring Eve's story to redemption.

My friend, later in this unit we will put together the stories that have built your structure and defined your identity. Please remember that nothing you have done or that was done to you is too big for God. Jesus paid it all. Every experience is part of your current narrative, but every experience does not have the power to define you or your destiny.

Body Image Blueprint

Now it's time to pray, process, and praise through what we just learned.

Let's Pray

Thank You, Father, for sending Jesus to be at the center of my life stories. Please bring to mind any structural stories that shaped me that You would like me to reassess. Jesus, I receive Your healing, mercy, forgiveness, love, and grace today. Amen.

Use the space provided to write your own prayer.

Pause to Process

1. Write about a defining moment that shaped your body image.

_____

_____

_____

_____

_____

_____

_____

2. Make a bullet-point list with words or phrases that remind you of this moment. (We will use these in this unit's Counselor's Cornerstone.)

_____

_____

_____

_____

_____

_____

_____

_____

_____

_____

_____

_____

Strong Foundation Verses

Use the following scriptural truths to strengthen your foundation. Consider saying them aloud, taking a picture of them to reference, or writing one that stands out on a sticky note and putting it somewhere you will see it daily.

- Jesus is our healer. (Isa. 53:5)
- Jesus is our redeemer. (Eph. 1:7)
- Jesus is our Savior. (John 3:16)
- Jesus is our teacher. (Ps. 32:8)
- Jesus is our friend. (Prov. 18:24)

Let's Rest in God's Word

As you complete this chapter's therapeutic coloring activity, meditate on the key verse and thank God for your body—exactly as it is today.

BY HIS WOUNDS WE ARE HEALED.

ISAIAH 53:5

Chapter 5

If Walls Could Talk

"Sometimes we see and hear her ghost in here." I will never forget those words spoken to me during a tour of the clinic we were considering buying when Matt graduated from chiropractic school. Chills ran down my spine as I thought about the woman who had passed away in that building. The tale was that she'd died decades earlier when the property had been her home, and even though this old house had since been turned into a place of business, she still liked to visit from time to time.

Despite the ghost tales, we did purchase that property. And thankfully, during the ten years we occupied that space, we never encountered any paranormal activity. But I would be lying if I said I didn't jump any time I was in the clinic after hours and heard even the slightest noise. The stories we'd been told permanently affected how we viewed and treated the building. I was so determined to stand our ground that I would walk around the outside of the building and pray for anything that didn't belong there to leave in Jesus' name. I never saw any ghosts leave, but I'm sure all those prayers were great for business!

In time, the Lord provided a new location that was bigger and ghost-story-free. We did have to remodel it to fit our business needs, at which time Matt wrote scriptures on the beams as an act of dedicating that space to the Lord. Instead of operating from a place of defense and praying out things that didn't belong, we were able to start on a firm foundation. But not all homes get the chance to be blessed from the beginning. If the walls could talk in many homes, they would tell stories of tragedy, trauma, and heartbreak.

Therapist Thoughts

An inner vow is often a promise we make to ourselves after being hurt or losing trust in someone. Though it feels like protection, it often brings more harm and barriers in relationships. Watch for words like *never* in your vocabulary to detect an inner vow.

Like any physical building, your body has a story to tell too. While most of us don't realize the effects previous generations have had on our body image, our bodies' lineage stories find ways to express themselves every day. The survey I conducted during graduate school asked more than a hundred women to identify the most significant influence on their view of their bodies. I was sure the answer would be culture. While culture did show up on some surveys, the recurring theme I saw on almost every survey was the influence of mothers, aunts, and sisters. Nearly every woman shared personal stories about hearing their moms or other female family members talk about how much they hated their bodies, needed to lose weight, or were on a new fad diet. Some women reported being put on a diet by their mothers as early as age seven. Story after story poured in from women whose view of their bodies was shaped negatively by their family members.

In this chapter's Body Image Blueprint section, you will get a chance to evaluate how your family upbringing affected your body image. But before we get there, I want to pause and share something I often remind my counseling clients of when looking at family dynamics. The purpose of analyzing how a family functions is not to cast blame or shame on any person. Instead, it serves to open our eyes to how things have been done so we can evaluate if that method is working and if it is a trait we want to pass on to our children.

With all my heart, I believe that most parents do the best they can with the skills they were taught. If you discover your family instilled negative body image views, please extend grace to them. No one taught them differently. The real enemy is Satan, not our family or any individual who negatively influenced our lives. But today, in Jesus' name, you can decide to break the generational curses of shame and insecurities.

One of my generational stories in body image lessons happened in one moment but took decades to undo. I was in high school, and a relative was instructing me on the ins and outs of dating. She looked me straight in the eyes and said, "Rachael, when you get married, if you don't want your husband to look at other women, then just keep your weight off."

She went on with her day, but that comment deposited a deep-rooted lie in the belly of my soul: that it was up to me to keep my future husband committed to our marriage. In that moment, as a teenager, I made an inner vow never to be overweight.

Now, this isn't a book on marriage, so we won't go into how wrong that line of thinking is, but let's look at it from a body image perspective. When I got married, not only did my weight matter to me because of worldly pressures, but it also became a symbol of my marriage success. The weight of that lie kept me in such bondage that I finally had to come clean with Matt about the pressure I was putting on myself to stay thin. It took me a while to put words to what I was feeling because, like many lies, it was buried so deep I wasn't aware I was operating from that unhealthy place.

In the mental health profession, it is often said that our thoughts affect our feelings and our feelings affect our behaviors. In this case, my irrational thoughts were causing me to feel and act completely out of line with God's Word.

> Every time we stand our ground in this area of body image, we break chains over ourselves and set free the generations to come.

As a mom of two girls, I have long wrestled with false beliefs that have been passed down from generation to generation. The generations before us simply taught us what they knew to be true from what they had learned in their cultures or families of origin. This is why I get excited when I see women standing up to pass on a different legacy. Every time we stand our ground in this area of body image, we break chains over ourselves and set free the generations to come. This is a battle worthy of the fight!

To change the narrative of what we pass on to the next generation is not easy. It will require intention and dedication. That's why I encourage you to remember that the unraveling of a distorted body image and the rebuilding of a body image that's in line with God's Word will take time.

As I write this book, I have a sticker on my desk that says, "Take one step at a time." Just as a house can't be built in a day, our view of body image cannot be rewired in a day. God will reveal one thing at a time so we can heal properly. Start to pay attention to your thoughts and beliefs around body image, and then challenge where they originated.

Here is the great news: change gets to start with you! Today marks a historic moment, when you say, "Enough is enough. As for me and my house, we will serve the Lord. Shame and defeat in this area of body image are gone with my generation."

Get excited, my friends. We are paving a new way for our daughters and the generations to come!

Temple Truths

The Bible places much importance on family lineage and the patterns that pass from generation to generation. One of the most frequently quoted of these generational passages is Exodus 20:5–6 in the Ten Commandments: "You shall not bow down to them [idols] or worship them; for I, the LORD your God, am a jealous God, punishing the children for the sin of the parents to the third and fourth generation of those who hate me, but showing love to a thousand generations of those who love me and keep my commandments."

The first part of that passage is a bit frightening, but as we read on, we see how simple God makes it for us to pass on a lineage of love. All we have to do is love Him, and out of that love comes a desire to keep His commandments. What a relief! The pressure is off to be perfect. We just need to love the Lord and let Him lead our family and generations to come.

While this all sounds great, I've been in ministry and counseling long enough to know that most women come from a lineage of pain and heartbreak. I have yet to meet a person who hasn't dealt with some level of pain from his or her family of origin. Even the healthiest families have some dysfunction because we are human beings and relationships are complicated.

But God's Word tells us that He will bless our generations. All we have to do is bring our pain to the feet of Jesus. This foundational truth applies to many areas, but for now, let's take a look at the generational iniquity of body image.

When Adam and Eve ate from the tree in the garden and had their eyes opened, their first response was to clothe themselves. But God stepped in to help: "The LORD God made garments of skin for Adam and his wife and clothed them" (Gen. 3:21).

Why would God make them clothes when they had already made some on their own? I believe it was because Adam and Eve tried to hide in their own strength, but the Lord knew it would never be enough. They needed His covering, just as we now need Jesus' blood covering our sins.

Adam's and Eve's decisions influenced generations. But God redeemed their mistakes and can do the same for our generational sins too. Remember, this problem is nothing new. Body image is a spiritual battle that started in the garden and ended on the cross.

Isaiah 61:4 tells us, "They will rebuild the ancient ruins and restore the places long devastated; they will renew the ruined cities that have been devastated for generations." And Joel 1:3 reminds us, "Tell it to your children, and let your children tell it to their children, and their children to the next generation."

I am so sorry if you've never had a family member stand up and break generational iniquities. My friend, God is asking *you* to stand up and be the one who begins rebuilding your family lineage.

> Start by receiving the reality that *your* body is good and God is good.

What good news do you need to share with your children about the faithfulness of God and the truth about their bodies? Start by receiving the reality that *your* body is good and God is good. Speak life over your body and the generations to come.

Body Image Blueprint

Now it's time to pray, process, and praise through what we just learned.

Let's Pray

Abba Father, thank You for my family. I am so grateful that even in their weakness and imperfections, You can restore and renew what the Enemy meant for evil. Reveal any generational sins or vows spoken over my body. In Jesus' name, I break the shame and addiction cycles in my family. I receive Your love, forgiveness, and blessing over my body. Amen.

Use the space provided to write your own prayer.

Pause to Process

1. Who has shaped how you view body image? Name both positive and negative influences.

_____

_____

_____

_____

_____

_____

2. Ask God to show you what generational beliefs about your body you might need to break, and write them here.

_____

_____

_____

_____

_____

_____

_____

_____

_____

_____

_____

_____

_____

_____

Strong Foundation Verses

Use the following scriptural truths to strengthen your foundation. Consider saying them aloud, taking a picture of them to reference, or writing one that stands out on a sticky note and putting it somewhere you will see it daily.

- "The LORD will rebuild." (Ps. 102:16)
- The Lord rebuilds better than before, with strong foundations. (Isa. 54:11)
- The Lord restores the fortunes of His people. (Amos 9:14 ESV)
- The Lord rebuilds, restores, and renews that which was devastated for generations. (Isa. 61:4)
- He is called the "Repairer of Broken Walls, Restorer of Streets with Dwellings." (Isa. 58:12)

Let's Rest in God's Word

This chapter's therapeutic activity is to create a *simple* genogram. Similar to a family tree, a genogram illustrates the connections between a person's family members.

We'll use the genogram to notice themes we don't want to pass on to the next generation, whether biological children or other younger people in your life who rely on you for mentorship or influence.

I've completed a sample genogram to help you fill in the blank template provided, but you may even want to work though this activity with a trusted friend or therapist.

As you work, note the following guidelines:

- Circles represent females.
- Squares represent males.
- If you do not know your ancestors, simply put a question mark in the coordinating box or circle.
- If you are not married, cross out the spouse.
- If you have more than one child or dependent, feel free to draw more.
- For the sake of this genogram, we are focusing only on body image and disordered eating. If you associate any family members with negative body image, disordered eating, or anything else in relation to the body, write *Yes* in the circle or square. Otherwise, write *No*.
- Because this is a simple genogram, there are not circles for aunts or siblings, but feel free to add those if any of those relationships affected your body image.
- You are welcome to elaborate as much or as little on this genogram as space permits.

- Finally, in the space provided, write generational body image themes you noticed, and pray for them to be broken, in Jesus' name.
- If you have children, write over the space for "child" any word the Lord brings to your mind as a symbol of the generational patterns you are breaking today. Examples include *restored*, *redeemed*, *healed*, *made new*, *set free*, and so on.

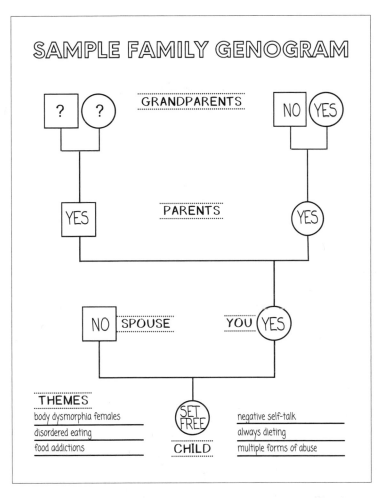

SAMPLE FAMILY GENOGRAM

GRANDPARENTS

? ? NO YES

PARENTS

YES YES

NO SPOUSE YOU YES

THEMES
body dysmorphia females
disordered eating
food addictions

SET FREE
CHILD

negative self-talk
always dieting
multiple forms of abuse

FAMILY GENOGRAM

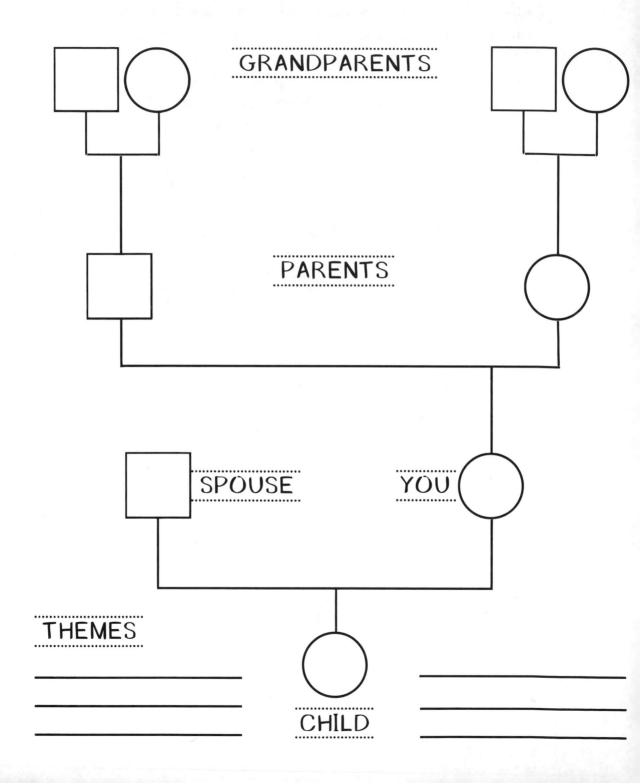

GRANDPARENTS

PARENTS

SPOUSE

YOU

THEMES

CHILD

Chapter 6

Hidden Hurt in the Closet

Now that I have three kids, I try to declutter our closets at least once a year, yet we still seem to accumulate So. Much. Junk. In fact, we have one closet I try to avoid completely because everything comes tumbling out when I dare to open it.

Can you relate?

As we do with the junk closets in our homes, many of us stuff our hurts so deep into the closets of our hearts that we don't even know what's in there anymore. Instead of dealing with the hurts, we avoid opening those doors at all costs.

Dealing with past wounds is a delicate issue to address, and I suspect this may be a challenging chapter for you to read. We are creating time and space to dive into topics that might be hard to discuss and could require some professional assistance.[*]

Remember, the Holy Spirit is with you as He brings these difficult issues into focus. He wants you to open that closet door in your heart and address all that "junk" that's been cluttering your life.

A problem I see in many resources that teach positive body image is that they don't consider the long-term effects that some forms of trauma may create. This can be especially true for body-based trauma, such as child sexual abuse (CSA).

According to Kneipp, Kelly, and Wise, several studies suggest that a strong link exists between trauma, body shame, and body image distortion (with further

---

[*] At the back of the book, you can find additional resources, including information that will point you to a therapist who can help you process your pain.

development of eating disorders).[1] Because this is only one chapter, not an entire book on the topic, we can't do a deep dive on trauma. However, in my experience counseling women with body image disorders, I often see some form of trauma that has kept my clients stuck in their pain. To be clear, trauma and pain are not always the cause of body image distortions, but they are linked frequently enough that it is worth exploring these closets in our hearts.

Trauma is an important topic that is often misunderstood. In my Eye Movement Desensitization and Reprocessing (EMDR) training, I learned much about trauma and its effects on the brain, body, and daily function.

The founder of EMDR, Francine Shapiro, shared the difference between "big *T*" trauma and "small *t*" trauma in her book *Eye Movement Desensitization and Reprocessing (EMDR) Therapy:*

> A "big T" trauma …, such as rape, sexual molestation, or combat experience, clearly has an impact on its victims in terms of how they behave, think, and feel about themselves, and in their susceptibility to pronounced symptoms, such as nightmares, flashbacks, and intrusive thoughts. These victims will have self-attributions such as "I'm powerless," "I'm worthless," or "I'm not in control." Of course, clients who have not experienced such traumas may also have dominant negative self-attributions, such as "I'm worthless," "I'm powerless," or "I'm going to be abandoned." Many of these clients seem to have derived their negative self-statements from early childhood experiences….
>
> Such clients were not, of course, blown up in a minefield or molested by a parent. Nevertheless, a memory of something that was said or that happened to them is locked in their brain and seems to have an effect similar to that of a traumatic experience. In fact, by dictionary definition, any event that has had a lasting negative effect on the self or psyche is by its nature "traumatic." Consequently, these ubiquitous adverse life events have long been referred to in EMDR practice as "small t" traumas.[2]

Therapist Thoughts

EMDR acts like a reset button for clients to reconnect to memories that once harbored intense feelings of shame, fear, and sorrow. The once-held belief that vulnerability is a weakness is replaced with growth, strength, and healing. (Dr. Mary Dainty)

Most people don't need to read a book or go to a licensed professional to learn they have experienced particular pain points in their past. But a therapist can help us open that closet door and sort through the junk we've been avoiding perhaps for far too long.

You may be asking, If we already know the wound is there, why do we avoid it?

I think there are a few reasons for this behavior.

First, as with those junk closets in my home, it's tempting to close the door on our pain with the hope of keeping it out of sight and out of mind. We believe that if we stuff a difficult issue deep enough, we can almost forget it's there and then it won't affect our daily lives.

Yet, just because we can't see something doesn't mean it isn't taking up space in our hearts and homes. I cringe when I walk past that chaotic closet because I know what's behind that door. I have even gone so far as to avoid that part of the house because I don't want to be reminded of the problem that I'm not ready to deal with.

While you might believe you can stuff your past wounds deep enough into your heart that you can't see them, I guarantee they still affect your life in more ways than one. Is there a particular topic you avoid discussing with your spouse or close friends? Do you avoid going to specific places or wearing certain pieces of clothing? Could those topics, places, or clothing articles be triggering something deep within you that you would rather avoid? Essentially, if you can't talk about it, it owns you.

Another reason I believe we stuff our trauma is that we genuinely don't know it's there. Our bodies and minds are simply amazing. In times of trauma, we have the ability to put up defense mechanisms that protect us. Yet, when the threat is gone, we can stay stuck in fight-or-flight mode, repressing painful memories as a defense mechanism to protect our fragile psyches. But eventually, sometimes decades later, there comes a point in our healing journey when the mind is ready to release those memories so they can be processed.

One of my personal "small t" traumas came to light in my marriage. From the moment we were married, I never liked to be naked in front of my husband. Matt had never done or said anything to make me feel shame around my body. But being seen in the nude felt weird and awkward. I attributed this to what I perceived as my body flaws and thought that if perhaps I could get in better shape, I would finally love to prance around the room in the buff.

After each pregnancy, I quickly lost weight and experienced multiple seasons in our marriage where I was in the best shape of my life. Yet I still avoided being seen naked and didn't like to be naked even if I was alone, like when stepping out of the shower.

> While you might believe you can stuff your past wounds deep enough into your heart that you can't see them, I guarantee they still affect your life in more ways than one.

One day, as I changed in my closet, I cried out to the Lord and asked Him why I couldn't stand being naked. He brought to my mind a memory from my childhood when a friend asked me to stay naked after we showered. At the time, I'd told her no and quickly dressed, but that experience had left me with an uneasy feeling in my stomach. Somehow, eight-year-old me knew this request was wrong, yet the experience brought shame and confusion around this idea of being naked.

Years later, when this old memory finally surfaced, I took this "new" information to my personal therapist, and we processed what that moment had imprinted in my young, impressionable brain. I didn't need to lose more weight or get in better shape to feel comfortable being naked in front of Matt. But I did need to lose the weight of that shame that had been lurking in the closet of my heart and affecting my relationship with my body and my spouse.

Perhaps the best description of "small *t*" traumas was given by my EMDR supervisor. She explained that "small *t*" trauma is like stacking tiny stones on top of one another. At first, that stone tower doesn't seem like a big deal. But over the years, as more stones are added, it gets so tall you can't see over it. In other words, you find yourself stuck and you can't figure out why.

As therapists, we are trying to find the original stone that was laid so we can get rid of the entire tower. The "small *t*" trauma I just shared with you regarding my shame about being naked had stones added to it multiple times throughout my life, from feeling awkward changing in the locker room to being called names based on my physical appearance. While none of these experiences appeared earth-shattering to those on the outside looking in, to me, each of these events left a mark on my brain that led me to believe "naked equals bad."

While I could tell you many stories of both "small *t*" and "big *T*" traumas I've experienced, I don't think that would be helpful to you. But I want you to know that you are not alone in having hidden hurts in your heart and that these trauma wounds have likely affected your body image. If God is bringing old wounds to your attention now, I encourage you to sit with Him in that place of pain and, if necessary, process it with a licensed counselor.

My friend Dr. Jon Chasteen writes in his book *Half the Battle*, "You can never tear down the walls of Jericho unless you first let God tear down the walls of your heart."[3] If you feel stuck on your body image journey, it might be time to tear down some walls in your heart so you can take the new territory that the Lord has given you.

Your body is not broken. But there might be some areas of your heart that need healing so you can begin to embrace new, healthy thoughts about your body.

Temple Truths

When we read the Bible, we don't see words like *trauma*, *emotional hurts*, *baggage*, or other terms that have recently become popular in the mental health community. Yet as I read those ancient stories, I imagine all the painful experiences those people must have deposited in their hearts and minds, especially when I see them showing up somewhere later in their life stories.

For example, I can only imagine how confusing it must have been to Adam and Eve when the Lord banished them from the garden in Genesis 3:23. Pain and trauma had just entered our fallen world, so God established a plan to bring healing and hope to future generations. But at the time, God's redirection to redeem what had been stolen from them probably just felt like rejection, especially as He sent Adam and Eve out of the garden.

The hero of that plan was Jesus. Not only did Jesus come to save our souls; He came to heal our wounds. Our Savior didn't just watch us experience pain; He walked through it Himself. Let's look at a *just a few* moments in Jesus' life when He personally experienced the pain of trauma:[4]

- From the moment Jesus was in His mother's womb, He experienced rejection, as Mary had to fight to protect His supernatural existence.
- Jesus' entrance into the world was less than glamourous—He was born in a manger, surrounded by barn animals.
- His life started out on the run and in hiding, because King Herod wanted Him dead.
- Jesus was rejected by the people of His time, which ultimately led to His death.
- Jesus experienced physical trauma as He was crucified. The night before His crucifixion in the garden of Gethsemane, He began to sweat blood, which experts believe is a sign of how much stress and trauma His body was experiencing.
- Jesus experienced emotional trauma as He was humiliated on the cross.
- Jesus experienced abandonment trauma as He cried out to His Father and asked why He had forsaken Him.

These are only a handful of painful moments Jesus encountered. He experienced tremendous pain, suffering, and heartbreak … all for you and me.

But Jesus not only experienced pain, He overcame it! He can sit with us in our trauma because He knows what it is like to suffer. And the best news is that He can also walk us out of it because of His sacrifice on the cross.

In Diane Langberg's book *Suffering and the Heart of God*, she says, "When we look at the resurrected Christ, what do we see? Scars."[5]

While we might have opted to be resurrected in a perfect body, Jesus *chose* to leave His scars! He no longer feels the pain of the scars, but they serve as a reminder to us that He is fully God, fully human, and fully with us in our pain.

Diane goes on to say, "The message of the scars in the resurrected Christ is not that the resurrection takes the suffering away, but rather that the resurrection catches it up into God's glory."[6]

First Peter 2:24 reminds us that in His own moment of trauma, Jesus bore our sins as well as the sins of those who inflicted pain upon us: "'He himself bore our sins' in his body on the cross, so that we might die to sins and live for righteousness; 'by his wounds you have been healed.'"

My friends, Jesus is our only source of hope in healing the deep wounds of our souls. Will you open those wounds to receive a healing touch from His scarred hands?

Body Image Blueprint

Now it's time to pray, process, and praise through what we just learned.

Let's Pray

Father, I know that no pain or trauma is too big for You to heal. Thank You for grieving and sitting with me in my pain. Draw near to me as I open my heart to clean out the hurt closets. Reveal anything You want to bring to the light, and then help me sort through it and remove it. Give me wisdom on seeking help, and surround me with people who can love me through this painful process. I trust You to comfort and heal me. In Jesus' name, amen.

Use the space provided to write your own prayer.

Pause to Process

1. Write about a "small *t*" trauma in your life.

_____

_____

_____

_____

_____

_____

2. How has that affected your body image?

_____

_____

_____

_____

_____

_____

_____

_____

_____

_____

_____

If "big *T*" traumas come to mind, please seek a licensed professional to help process them.

Strong Foundation Verses

Use the following scriptural truths to strengthen your foundation. Consider saying them aloud, taking a picture of them to reference, or writing one that stands out on a sticky note and putting it somewhere you will see it daily.

- God comforts us in our troubles. (2 Cor. 1:3–4)
- He is with us through the darkest valleys. (Ps. 23:4)
- "Blessed are those who mourn, for they will be comforted." (Matt. 5:4)
- He will uphold you with His righteous right hand. (Isa. 41:10)
- He will wipe away every tear from your eyes. (Rev. 21:4)

Let's Rest in God's Word

As you complete this chapter's therapeutic coloring activity, meditate on the key verse and thank God for being near to the brokenhearted.

THE LORD IS
CLOSE TO THE
BROKENHEARTED
AND SAVES
THOSE WHO ARE
CRUSHED IN
SPIRIT.

PSALM 34:18

Unit 2 Counselor's Cornerstone

Strengthening Your Foundation

The Bible gives us entire chapters detailing the familial lineage across historical generations. Because these genealogical details can be cumbersome and complicated (if not a little boring to read), scholars have found it helpful to chart the generational themes along a timeline.

Timelines are powerful because they show us how significant events shape a person's life. Even Jesus had a timeline of events that brought Him to His destination on the cross (and beyond). While some of these events may have seemed insignificant when they happened, when we look at the whole timeline, we can see God's hand on His life at each step.

Before we make your body image timeline, let's look at a few timelines in the Bible.

1. Read the story of Eve (Gen. 2:18—4:26). In the space provided, create a brief timeline of her life. Highlight or circle any events that likely made a significant impact on her. Can you relate to her highlighted moments?

2. Read the story of Mary (Luke 1:26–56; 2:1–21). In the space provided, create a brief timeline of her life. Highlight or circle any events that likely made a significant impact on her. Can you relate to her highlighted moments?

3. Read about or reflect on the life of Jesus. (You can find Him throughout the Bible, but a great place to start is in the Gospels: Matthew, Mark, Luke, or John.) In the space below, create a brief timeline of His life. Feel free to use any of the moments mentioned from His life in chapter 6. Highlight or circle any events that likely made a significant impact on Him and His ministry. Write any significant events you see on Jesus' timeline, such as when He *healed*, *set free*, *spoke life*, and so on. We will use these words on *your* timeline.

Counselor's Chat

In the unit 2 video, I'm speaking life and healing over your body. I will walk you through this timeline activity, offer a special prayer over your body image timeline, and offer additional resources for healing trauma-based wounds. You can access the video with the QR code on page 22.

Therapy Toolbox

Now that we've studied the timelines of a few individuals in the Bible, let's make *your* body image timeline. I've included an example timeline to get you started. Notice there are both negative and positive experiences on the timeline.

Begin by listing your key timeline moments in the space provided.

Start at birth. Then add critical moments in your body image journey. These may include pivotal experiences, such as puberty, weight gain, weight loss, pregnancy, sickness, trauma, or anything that comes to mind when you think of your body. More memories may surface as you continue to read this book. When they do, just jump back here and add them to your timeline.

Next, write a word or phrase that comes to mind for each season. Example: *I felt thin, put on weight, boys started noticing me*, and so on. Look for themes along your body image timeline. Ask the Holy Spirit to show you if any of the boxes were of significance. Did any lies enter that season that need to be confronted and put on trial? (We will do that in our next Counselor's Cornerstone.)

If this practice feels overwhelming or if any traumatic memories are on your timeline, please seek professional help to guide you through it.

With your body image timeline complete, look back on the words you wrote about Jesus' timeline. Write those words over your body image timeline.

Let your timeline serve as a tool to help you notice themes and events that have shaped how you view your body. Remember, because of what Jesus did on the cross, those old beliefs do not have the final say. Declare yourself free in the name of Jesus.

BODY TIMELINE

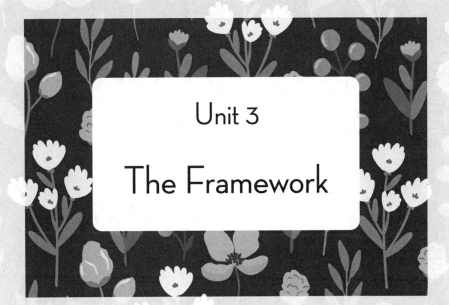

Unit 3

The Framework

Chapter 7

Thoughts Are the Foreman

In 2017, God dropped it on my heart to run a marathon. As soon as the idea entered my mind, I immediately dismissed it. Surely there was no way God was calling *me* to run a marathon. I went on with my day, but that idea to run a marathon came back into my thoughts. Finally, I shouted, "No, God, I will not run a marathon. Remember, I am not a runner!" To which He politely replied, "Who told you that you aren't a runner?"

I was busted.

Therapist Thoughts

When confronted with a defeating thought, ask:
1. What would I do if *this* defeating thought weren't true?
2. What would I do if I weren't afraid?

The thought that I wasn't a runner had stemmed from my first attempts at running with the track team as an adolescent. Do you recall the story I shared earlier in the book about being so slow my teammates had packed up and left by the time I arrived back at the starting line? That's only the beginning of the many experiences that confirmed the belief that I am NOT a runner. My track coach would put me in the last heat, filled with the slowest runners. I always came in dead last, even in that slow heat.

Still, all those years later, God kept saying, "Rachael, you can run a marathon." So, after much prayer, I decided to sign up for my first—and only—marathon. I joined a local running group, and every Saturday we would meet for our long runs. In the first run, they put us in groups with other people who ran at similar paces. As we began our run, the coach in my group came alongside me and said, "Rachael, you have got to breathe. If you can't hold a conversation at this pace, you will never make these long distances."

It turned out I was in the wrong group. I could not hold a conversation at that pace, so they moved me to a slower group. That was pivotal in my running experience because it taught me that running could be enjoyable if I chose my pace wisely.

Training for that marathon became one of the most challenging yet rewarding experiences in my life. In fact, during my long runs, God began to speak to me about writing this book. Step by step, He was tackling yet another disqualifying thought, since I'd long believed I could never be a writer. Why? Because English was not my strong subject in school. But through His guidance, I learned that just as running that marathon took one step at a time, writing this book has come one step of faith at a time. I believe He'd asked me to run that marathon not to burn calories or so I could brag about the distance covered; instead, God had led me to run that marathon to break down strongholds in my thoughts that were holding me back in many areas of my life.

On race day, I started slow, held a conversational pace, and ran the race set before me. I still remember the people who cheered us on at the beginning and the end of the race with signs, banners, and cold beverages. I did notice, however, that few people were cheering for us in the middle stretch of that marathon. It was in those middle unseen miles that I had to dig deep into my thoughts and remember why I'd started the race to begin with. Otherwise, I would have never made it to the finish line.

While I will never make an Olympic career out of running, the pace at which I run does not disqualify me, or you, from being a runner. The most important lesson I learned from running that marathon was the power of my thoughts. Where your mind goes, your life will follow.

The false belief that I was not a runner had kept me from saying yes to races throughout much of my adult life. Time and again, I had immediately disqualified myself before the race ever began. That's why this chapter on self-discipline in our thoughts is crucial for us to be victorious in our body image journeys. Much as a foreman directs the workers during the construction of a home, our thoughts really do guide our lives.

Let's look at what God's Word says about taking our thoughts captive.

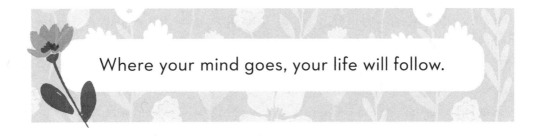

Where your mind goes, your life will follow.

Temple Truths

The idea that we have power over our thoughts was one I didn't always know or apply to my life. I was in my early twenties when I first had the "Aha!" moment about my thoughts. I shared with Matt a thought I had been wrestling with, and he said something I will never forget: "Rach, just change the channel if you don't like what's playing in your mind."

We have the power to "change the channel" of our thoughts, but the choice is only ours to make. Today, the comparison may be easily explained as scrolling by something on social media. Scrolling past unhealthy thoughts is not the same as ignoring them; rather, it is choosing which thoughts we want to meditate on in that moment. Just keep scrolling by the thoughts that don't bring you life. And in time, the algorithm will shift and your feed will look entirely different from when you first started. YOUR choices decide what you receive!

Shortly after that moment when I realized I could choose my own thoughts and therefore choose my own outcomes, I discovered Joyce Meyer's book *Battlefield of the Mind*.[1] That's when I got to work on learning how and why to take my thoughts captive. While we can scroll by some thoughts, others that are more deeply embedded might need to be cross-examined.

I love when the worlds of science and faith collide, which is precisely what happened as I studied the Bible alongside psychological theories regarding this topic of thoughts. We know there is nothing new under the sun (see Eccl. 1:9), and as Christians, we believe the Bible is the original source for any and all truth by which we live. One of my favorite scriptures about thoughts comes from Paul's teachings in 2 Corinthians 10:5: "We demolish arguments and every pretension that sets itself up against the knowledge of God, and we take captive every thought to make it obedient to Christ."

The word that draws me into that verse is *captive*. Notice how it doesn't say to get rid of or ignore the thought. It clearly says to take it *captive*.

Have you ever observed a scene in a movie during which a prisoner of war is taken captive? Usually, that prisoner is tortured and tested to uncover strategic information. We need to do the same with any body image thoughts that are not from God. Tie them up, look them in the eye, and ask where they came from and what they intend to do to you. It is more powerful to stop and tackle one thought at a time than to ignore the thoughts. Ignoring thoughts doesn't make them go away. It temporarily silences them. But even in their silence, they are still directing your life.

A practical tip for knowing whether a thought is from God when you take it captive is to see what fruit it produces. If it is life-giving, it is from God. If it robs you of your joy, peace, energy, or other fruit of the Spirit, it is from the Enemy. Any thought that disempowers you is not from the Lord.

I knew the idea to run a marathon—and to write this book—was from the Lord because the result of both of those thoughts was life-giving. The belief that I am not a runner disempowered me, so it was from the Enemy or my self-defeating inner voice.

Now that we've seen proof that God cares deeply about our thoughts, let's look at how science views them. In counseling, a common theory practiced by many therapists is cognitive behavioral therapy (CBT). Counselors who use this theoretical orientation believe that to change one's behaviors, we must first change their thoughts. Simply put, your thoughts affect your feelings, and your feelings affect your behaviors. For example, if you think your worth is in your weight, the feeling that follows might be shame about your weight, and a possible behavior would be to obsess over your weight or neglect your body. This is known as the Cognitive Triangle,[2] but I refer to it as the Triangle Effect.

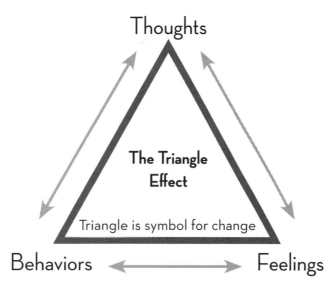

Growing up, I was an algebra nerd. I competed in state competitions for algebraic equations, and I tested out of my college math classes when I was a junior in high school. When I first saw this concept of thoughts-feelings-behaviors in graduate school, my brain immediately visualized it as the Greek letter used in algebra to represent change. It is pronounced "delta," and it looks like a triangle.

Isn't that interesting? If we want to see lasting change, we must activate all three areas of this triangle—not just the thoughts but also the feelings and behaviors.

This is why it's not enough for me to tell you to love your body (which is a feeling). We must get to the root thoughts, or beliefs, that are causing the disconnection between your mind, soul, body, and spirit.

We will discuss feelings in the next chapter, but for now let's head back to the Bible to look at a few different situations when Satan tried to mess with people's thoughts.

Of course, the first time we witness it is when he approached Eve in the garden. I extend so much grace to Eve because (like any of us) she didn't know what she didn't know. If Eve had learned to take her thoughts captive, maybe she wouldn't have entered into conversation with Satan in the first place. In Genesis 3, we see Satan present Eve with a thought that led her down the wrong path: "Did God really say you must not eat the fruit from any of the trees in the garden?" (v. 1 NLT).

At first, Eve stood her ground. She replied to the serpent, "Of course we may eat fruit from the trees in the garden.... It's only the fruit from the tree in the middle of the garden that we are not allowed to eat. God said, 'You must not eat it or even touch it; if you do, you will die'" (vv. 2–3 NLT).

Satan responded, "You won't die!" (v. 4 NLT).

And Eve was convinced.

In this short dialogue between Eve and Satan, we see that by allowing Satan to shift her thoughts, Eve was propelled into taking action and opening a door that God did not want her to walk through.

Remember that Paul brought up this encounter between Eve and Satan in his teachings in 2 Corinthians 11:3–4, "But I fear that somehow your pure and undivided devotion to Christ will be corrupted, just as Eve was deceived by the cunning ways of the serpent. You happily put up with whatever anyone tells you, even if they preach a different Jesus than the one we preach, or a different kind of Spirit than the one you received, or a different kind of gospel than the one you believed" (NLT).

Satan didn't stop with Eve. Here are two times we see him use people to mess with thoughts in the Bible:

- In Matthew 16:22–23, we see Satan try to use a friend to disrupt thoughts and beliefs: "Peter took him aside and began to rebuke him. 'Never, Lord!' he said. 'This shall never happen to you!' Jesus turned and said to Peter, 'Get behind me, Satan! You are a stumbling block to me.'"
- In Job 2:9–10, we see Job's wife try to change his thoughts, or beliefs, toward God: "His wife said to him, 'Are you still maintaining your integrity? Curse God and die!' He replied, 'You are talking like a foolish woman. Shall we accept good from God, and not trouble?'"

And then, we see Satan speak directly to Jesus in Matthew 4 when He was led into the wilderness to be tested. Multiple times Satan challenged Jesus' thoughts, or beliefs, about who He was: "The tempter came to him and said, 'If you are the Son of God, tell these stones to become bread'" (v. 3). Every time Satan challenged what Jesus knew to be true, Jesus boldly put the accuser back in his lowly place.

Satan knows the power of our thoughts, and he continues to persuade us to believe something is missing or wrong with our bodies—the very bodies designed and created by God. Or, in the words of Paul, Satan deceives us into thinking the gospel and Jesus aren't enough to cover everything, including our body shame.

> Every time Satan challenged what Jesus knew to be true, Jesus boldly put the accuser back in his lowly place.

Body Image Blueprint

Now it's time to pray, process, and praise through what we just learned.

Let's Pray

Father, thank You for giving me the power to take my thoughts captive and make them obedient to Christ. Please reveal any thoughts about my body that are not from You. Renew my mind in Jesus' name. Amen.

Use the space provided to write your own prayer.

Pause to Process

1. What thought(s) come to mind about your body? Write one or more in the space provided.

2. Add a positive or negative sign beside each thought to indicate whether each belief has a positive or negative impact on your life at this time.

We will use one of these thoughts in the Counselor's Cornerstone activity at the end of this unit.

Strong Foundation Verses

Use the following scriptural truths to strengthen your foundation. Consider saying them aloud, taking a picture of them to reference, or writing one that stands out on a sticky note and putting it somewhere you will see it daily.

- Think on things that are worthy of praise. (Phil. 4:8)
- "Give careful thought to the paths for your feet." (Prov. 4:26)
- Jesus asked, "Why do you entertain evil thoughts in your hearts?" (Matt. 9:4)
- "Fix your thoughts on Jesus." (Heb. 3:1)
- "The Word of God … judges the thoughts and attitudes of the heart." (Heb. 4:12)
- Let the Spirit renew your thoughts. (Eph. 4:23)

Let's Rest in God's Word

As you complete this chapter's therapeutic coloring activity, meditate on the key verse and thank God for your body—exactly as it is today.

TAKE CAPTIVE EVERY THOUGHT

WE DEMOLISH ARGUMENTS AND EVERY PRETENSION THAT
SETS ITSELF UP AGAINST THE KNOWLEDGE OF GOD,
AND WE TAKE CAPTIVE EVERY THOUGHT
TO MAKE IT OBEDIENT TO CHRIST.
2 CORINTHIANS 10:5

Chapter 8

The Creaky Floorboards

Good friends of ours recently built a new home, and the first day they moved in, they noticed their new floors creaked when they walked on them. They let their contractor know, but he assured them that the floors would settle in and all would be well. In other words, they were instructed to ignore the problem and wait for it to fix itself.

Fast-forward six months, and not only were the floors still creaking, but they had gotten worse.

Their builders finally assessed the situation and determined that the floors had indeed been installed incorrectly. Our sweet friends had to move all their furniture out of their new home and get the floors reinstalled. Needless to say, this was not what they had envisioned when they moved into their dream home.

Those creaky floorboards are much like the emotions in our hearts. We usually try to ignore the creaks, hoping they'll settle in and grow quiet in time.

Emotions have gotten a bad reputation in our society, especially in Christian culture. As a counselor, I believe emotions are neither good or bad, but some are definitely more comfortable than others. They can be noisy and cause confusion when ignored. I see them much like a warning light on our car when it instructs us to check the engine. We can choose to cover them up with a sticky note, like my old college roommate used to do, or get the car inspected by an expert. Either way, the problem that caused the light to come on (or the emotion to surface) is still there, and it's not going to settle in and fix itself.

Do you remember how I shared with you in the introduction about when I first confessed to someone that I had a problem with my body? If you skimmed that part, here's a brief recap, but this time, instead of the story's details, let's look at the emotions that arose. I've *italicized* the emotions in parentheses throughout the story.

> Emotions have a way of letting us know what's happening in our hearts if we will stop long enough to listen.

I was a sophomore in college when I told my small group leader at church about my struggles. (I felt the *courage* to speak up here.) It was the first time I'd told anyone about my body issues, and I could tell by the stunned look on her face that she was ready to call someone for help. I quickly assured her that I had found my way to freedom and was just offering a testimony of what I had already overcome. (I felt *fear*, *shame*, and *embarrassment*. In other words, I minimized my emotions to diffuse the situation.)

Much to my surprise, the next week, I received a phone call from my college pastor. (I felt *shocked*, *surprised*, and *angry* at myself for speaking up.) He let me know that the leader had shared my "testimony" with him and that he would like me to share it with my college peers—nearly a thousand students! (I felt *betrayed* by my leader for sharing my story without my permission.) In my head, I was screaming, *Nope, nope, nope … Can't you all see I am STILL in this struggle?!* (I felt *unseen* and *unheard*.)

I managed to politely decline by letting him know I was not a public speaker. (I felt *panic,* which made me retreat.) He told me to pray about it, to which I agreed, but I never did bring the topic up to God. (I felt *distant* from God because, to avoid the issue, I had to avoid talking to Him.) Instead, I dodged my campus pastor and life group leader that entire semester for fear they would somehow wrestle me to the microphone. (I felt *lonely*.)

While I am finally picking up the microphone and writing this book nearly two decades later, that experience taught me something about emotions that I had to spend time unlearning. My nineteen-year-old self had learned that if you share how you feel about your body, you might be met with judgment or well-meaning people who tell you to walk around the emotions. When we walk around emotions, it's like we are putting a sticky note on the check engine light of our heart. Emotions have a way of letting us know what's happening in our hearts if we will stop long enough to listen.

The church tells us we shouldn't care about our external appearance while the world tells us to obsess over it. I don't believe either of these extremes is a healthy or realistic way to live. I could tell you to love your body, but that's just me telling you how to feel. While I want all of us to embrace our bodies, we can't get there by stepping around emotions.

Wherever you fall on this spectrum of extremes, emotions often drive our motivations. Dr. Cassie Reid, one of my college counseling professors, taught us to lean into emotions instead of walking around them. Leaning in simply means listening to what the emotions are trying to tell us. Emotions serve as the creaking floors of our home, warning us that something deeper needs to be addressed. We must pay attention.

The floors of your heart are creaking around this area of your body image for a reason. Don't ignore the feelings. Instead, invite the Lord to help you examine the underlying cause of the emotions. And then allow space in your heart and life to work on the repairs.

Therapist Thoughts

When a client pinpoints an emotion she is experiencing, I often ask, "Where do you feel that emotion in your body?" Sit for a moment, take three deep breaths, scan your body from head to toe, and notice where you feel any emotion.

Temple Truths

This topic of stuffing emotions is something I have struggled with most of my life in more areas than just body image. How we handle things in one area of our lives is often how we handle them in all areas.

A few years ago, I graded one of my daughter's homework assignments for school. It was a vocabulary assignment, and one of her words was *harbor*. She was to complete the sentence that began, "I sometimes harbor thoughts about …"

Her answer stopped me in my grading tracks: "How mad I am at people." My sweet girl was only ten years old at the time, but she'd already learned to stuff emotions when they seemed wrong or overwhelming.

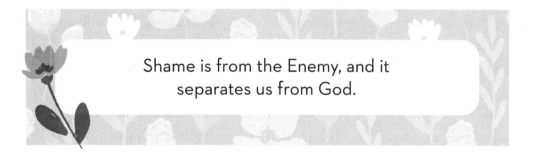

Shame is from the Enemy, and it separates us from God.

At first, I thought she might have learned this unhealthy behavior pattern from me, as I was just starting to learn how to process and share my emotions in healthy ways. But then I realized that hiding from scary feelings is innate in our fallen world.

In Genesis 3:7, after the fall, we see Adam and Eve innately knew to hide when they felt shame: "At that moment their eyes were opened, and they suddenly felt shame at their nakedness. So they sewed fig leaves together to cover themselves" (NLT).

You see? Hard emotions were already being hidden in the garden of Eden. Adam and Eve *felt shame* and hid. In other words, they felt an uncomfortable emotion and then took action. But from what we can read in the Bible, they didn't acknowledge, voice, discuss, or process the way they were feeling at the time.

I find it interesting that shame was one of the first emotions we see enter the world after the fall. Shame is from the Enemy, and it separates us from God.

Shame is one of the biggest struggles most women encounter in their body image battle. While I can't wave a magic wand and make your shame disappear (oh, how I wish I could!), Jesus *can* lift the shame off your shoulders—and that's the real weight you need to lose.

The thing is, we have a choice. We can either listen to our feelings and run to God with them, or we can hide our feelings in shame and run away from Him (and from other people who love us).

In the Bible, we see Mary, the mother of Jesus, process her emotions well when the angel Gabriel approached to tell her the news of being chosen to birth the Savior of our world. Luke 1:29 says Mary was *"confused and disturbed"* (NLT) about what this news could mean. Instead of hiding from those emotions, as we saw with Adam and Eve, Mary pressed in to learn more. After Mary and the angel went back and forth in dialogue, with the angel assuring her that she need not fear, Mary let go of shame and fear and *accepted* what was about to happen: "'I am the Lord's servant,' Mary answered. 'May your word to me be fulfilled.' Then the angel left her" (Luke 1:38).

Now is a great time to pause and reflect on what we just read in God's Word. Adam and Eve felt shame and hid, which separated them from God. Mary felt confused and disturbed, but instead of running away or hiding, she processed her emotions and embraced what the angel had told her, letting's God's guidance shape her thoughts and then her actions. Mary's choice brought unity within herself and reestablished her (and later our) union with the Lord.

The Enemy loves when we hide not only from our emotions but from the Lord. He knows if he can cause us to fear the emotions that come up, we will run *away* from the Lord instead of *to* Him.

Emotions are not something we need to hide from, yet in order to stop and embrace them, we must normalize them. The Bible is full of stories that illustrate the emotions people felt. Here are just a few of the emotions some heroes of the Bible felt:

- Moses burned with *anger* (Ex. 11:8).
- Jacob felt great *fear* and *distress* (Gen. 32:7).
- Jonathan burned with *anger* and was *crushed* in spirit (1 Sam. 20:34 NLT).

- King David was filled with *joy* (1 Chron. 29:9 NLT).
- Esther felt *distress* (Est. 4:4).

Just as these heroes of the faith felt a broad range of emotions, we too are wired to feel. It's all part of our divine design. We often avoid feeling out of fear that we can't control our emotions. However, the more we practice feeling and expressing emotions, the more we give them an outlet to be expressed in a healthy way.

As we take time to process these emotions around body image, see if your innate response is to run *to* or *from* the Lord. There is no right or wrong answer here, but it may be time to turn your heart and emotions back to God in this area of body image.

Body Image Blueprint

Now it's time to pray, process, and praise through what we just learned.

Let's Pray

Abba, thank You for creating emotions that always speak to me about what's going on in my heart. I confess that I don't always run to You with my emotions. Please show me what's at the root of the feelings around my body. Restore my union with You and with my body. In Jesus' name, amen.

Use the space provided to write your own prayer.

Pause to Process

1. Take time to examine the specific emotions you're feeling about your body. Allow yourself to feel, and don't try to hide them. Try writing in a journal to record your feelings each day. Which feeling do you have most about your body? Which feeling is the hardest for you to express?

_____

_____

_____

_____

_____

2. Remember in the last chapter when we learned that your thoughts affect your feelings and your feelings affect your behaviors? What thoughts are lying beneath your emotions? Take time to see what truths the Lord wants to reveal.

_____

_____

_____

_____

_____

_____

_____

_____

_____

_____

_____

_____

_____

_____

_____

_____

_____

_____

_____

_____

_____

_____

_____

_____

_____

_____

Strong Foundation Verses

Use the following scriptural truths to strengthen your foundation. Consider saying them aloud, taking a picture of them to reference, or writing one that stands out on a sticky note and putting it somewhere you will see it daily.

- Scripture offers a prayer to restore the joy of your salvation. (Ps. 51:12)
- The Lord comforts and restores joy and gladness. (Isa. 51:3)
- The Lord replaces beauty for ashes, joy for mourning, and praise for despair. (Isa. 61:3)
- "Do not be afraid; you will not be put to shame." (Isa. 54:4)
- Jesus weeps with us. (John 11:35)

Let's Rest in God's Word

When helping my clients identify their emotions, I like to use a tool called the **emotion wheel** (created by psychologist Robert Plutchik).[1] The purpose behind this tool is to help identify unique emotions that stem from core emotions that you might not yet have words to express. Instead of using the emotion wheel, we are going to do something similar, but with flowers.

Use the emotion flowers on the next page to give voice to things you might feel concerning your body. Color each flower a different color, and pay attention to the emotions listed on each petal. Add an extra design or special color to any of the emotions that resonate with you. I encourage you to refer to the emotion flowers as needed throughout your healing journey.

Chapter 9

When Building Is Delayed

When constructing a new home, the building process often gets delayed. A shortage of supplies or unexpected rain can leave the crew unable to work. Watching the timeline get pushed back by days, weeks, and even months can be maddening, which is why most contractors wisely remind customers to expect these turns in the project.

I wish more people talked about unrealistic expectations regarding our bodies. Let me be clear: *your body is not a project*, but often we go into a new diet or exercise plan as if it were.

One of my first experiences treating my body like a project was during my sophomore year of college. My sister and I had committed to a forty-day fitness program that required before and after pictures and measurements. Like many extreme fitness plans, it only made my disordered eating worse. I methodically followed every detail in the program guide. In the end, I had gained eight pounds, developed an increased appetite for food, and become even more frustrated with my body for, yet again, letting me down.

Let's just say there were no "after" pictures from that program.

Recently, when my sister and I were cleaning out our childhood rooms, we came across our sad, staged "before" pictures that never did deliver the happy ending we'd worked so hard to achieve.

In hindsight, I'm so thankful that all the quick-fix diet plans have failed me. Otherwise, I would feel the temptation to take credit for how I look and put my worth in my ability to carry out a diet or exercise plan.

We are now through half the chapters in this book, and it's time to talk about what most people expect to learn from any diet, fitness, or body image book: *behavior modification*.

Most counselors agree that behavior modification isn't a long-term solution to a problem. This is why most diets fail. If someone is addicted to sugar, instructing her to stop eating it will only work for so long. To make lasting change, we must address the root cause of the behavior.

We've already addressed the way our thoughts affect our feelings and our feelings affect our behaviors. Now it's time to delay building our body image home so we can take a closer look at the behavioral part of that triangle effect.

Therapist Thoughts

The diet industry puts a lot of effort into trying to help people change their habits through willpower and behavioral modifications. This top-down approach can be helpful for some people, but many people end up disillusioned, chasing one diet fad after another, because behavior modification alone is like trimming the top of a weed without getting all the roots.

In contrast, a bottom-up approach addresses the root issues below the surface. With this approach, we switch directions, stop, take a deep breath, and invite God to show us His view of our bodies to make space for behaviors that come from our Creator's core beliefs. (Adapted from Dr. Shannon Crawford)

Let's ponder some thoughts about your behaviors. Before you make a decision about food, exercise, or body image, ask yourself these questions:

- Does this behavior glorify God in my body?
- Is there any sin in this behavior?
- Are there any unhealthy thoughts or motives directing this behavior?
- Do I hide this behavior?
- Is this behavior something I want to pass on to the next generation?

Each chapter of this book reveals different layers that must be addressed as we rebuild our body image. It's okay to delay the rebuilding to allow time for the Holy Spirit to speak truth about our behavior.

Remember, your body is precisely where it needs to be today. If you feel frustrated with the journey, stop, exhale, and trust the process.

Temple Truths

Questions I get asked about body image include, but aren't limited to, the following:

- What's a healthy weight for my body type?
- Is it okay to weigh myself daily?
- Should I count calories or carbohydrates?
- Do I really need to exercise every day?
- What do you consider overexercising?

These, along with more intimate questions, have one thing in common: behavior. Here is my question back to those women and you:

What is that behavior providing for you?

Let's be clear: not all behaviors are wrong. Behaviors become toxic only when we base our identity in them. That's when they have such a stronghold on us that they can become "the boss" of our lives. The behaviors decide what we do, when we do it, and how much money we spend on it. Toxic behaviors left unbridled become addictions.

This lack of self-control is described in Proverbs 25:28: "Like a city whose walls are broken through is a person who lacks self-control." This seems fitting in our unit as we discuss the framework—because without this self-control, the beams that are holding your body image home together will collapse.

However, it's essential that we don't use Bible verses to justify our obsessive behaviors. At the time of writing this book, I am a few pant sizes bigger than when I first set out to write a book on body image. I love the timing of the Lord, because if I had written this book many years ago, when I was lighter and in better physical shape, I would have likely done damage with my words by using scripture to justify my struggles with orthorexia.

> Toxic behaviors left unbridled become addictions.

According to the Center for Discovery Eating Disorder Treatment, "Orthorexia is an eating disorder characterized by having an unsafe obsession with healthy food. An obsession with healthy dieting and consuming only 'pure foods' or 'clean eating' becomes deeply rooted in the individual's way of thinking to the point that it interferes with their daily life."[1]*

As noted earlier, there is nothing wrong with healthy eating—until it becomes so deeply rooted in our way of thinking that it interferes with daily living. Eating healthy, whole foods is a good thing, but we must be careful to keep it from becoming our god.

To gain a biblical perspective of our behaviors, we must look at the spirit driving the behavior rather than the behavior itself. No, you won't find direct answers in the Bible about some body image behaviors, though Proverbs 11:1 does make me giggle: "The LORD detests dishonest scales, but accurate weights find favor with him." And, no, it is not refer-ring to your "dishonest" bathroom scale. Here is a simple question to ask yourself about

---

*   For a brief overview on eating disorders, please turn to the Resources at the end of the book

your body image behaviors that we see throughout the Bible: *Is my behavior being driven by faith or fear?*

One of my favorite chapters in the entire Bible is Hebrews 11. The phrase "by faith" is repeated more than twenty times in one chapter! The chapter starts by describing faith: "The fundamental fact of existence is that this trust in God, this faith, is the firm foundation under everything that makes life worth living. It's our handle on what we can't see. The act of faith is what distinguished our ancestors, set them above the crowd" (vv. 1–2 MSG).

Here are just a few of those "by faith" moments noted in Hebrews 11:

- *"By faith* we understand the universe was formed at God's command." (v. 3)
- *"By faith* Abel brought God a better offering than Cain did. " (v. 4)
- *"By faith* Noah, when warned about things not yet seen,… built an ark to save his family." (v. 7)
- *"By faith* Abraham, when called to go to a place he would later receive as his inheritance, obeyed and went, even though he did not know where he was going." (v. 8)
- *"By faith* he made his home in the promised land like a stranger in a foreign country.… For he was looking forward to the city **with foundations, whose architect and builder is God**." (vv. 9–10)

I highly encourage you to take time to read Hebrews 11 for yourself and highlight all the "by faith" moments. But can you believe what we just read in Hebrews 11:10? I bolded it above so you don't miss it. By faith, Abraham was willing to follow the Lord because *he recognized the value of having a city built on a solid foundation, whose architect and builder is God*. A body image home built on God's foundation with Him as the architect and builder is a home that can withstand anything the Enemy brings our way.

The opposite of faith is fear. God knew we would wrestle with choosing faith over fear. In fact, we see the word *fear* in the NIV translation 336 times. It's important to notice two types of fear represented here: fear of God and fear of man.

Fear of God is good and commanded of us in Deuteronomy 6:13: "Fear the LORD your God, serve him only and take your oaths in his name."

In contrast, we read in Proverbs 29:25, "Fear of man will prove to be a snare, but whoever trusts in the LORD is kept safe."

> A body image home built on God's foundation with Him as the architect and builder is a home that can withstand anything the Enemy brings our way.

With the exception of trauma-based behaviors, most distorted body image behaviors are rooted in fear of man. Considering those, let's look at the difference in behaviors driven by faith versus fear:

- By faith, I choose to eat whole foods, even if I don't lose weight, because I know the benefits to my unseen body.
- By fear, I count every calorie that enters my mouth and overexercise when I feel guilty for food eaten.

- By faith, I move my body according to what it needs that day.
- By fear, I force my body to perform past the point of discomfort and into pain.

- By faith, I decide not to weigh myself every day.
- By fear, I let the number on the scale determine my mood and direction for the day.

Please note, these faith-versus-fear illustrations are examples. I hesitate to tell you specific behaviors that are good for you. Only you and the Lord know your heart and your needs. As 1 Corinthians 10:23 reminds us, "'I have the right to do anything,' you say—but not everything is beneficial. 'I have the right to do anything'—but not everything is constructive."

Because of your free will, you have the right to do anything. But only you can decide if it's beneficial to your body, soul, spirit, and life.

I leave you with this charge, which was initially given to Joshua as he decided between choosing faith or fear: "Have I not commanded you? Be strong and courageous. Do not be afraid; do not be discouraged, for the LORD your God will be with you wherever you go" (Josh. 1:9).

My friend, I know it's not easy letting go of some behaviors that have become your identity. Choose faith today as you let go of any behaviors driven by fear.

Body Image Blueprint

Now it's time to pray, process, and praise through what we just learned.

Let's Pray

Father, by faith, I choose to believe You have a plan for my life. You have plans to prosper and not harm me, plans for hope and a future. By faith, I choose to walk in that plan. I lay down any pride, shame, or fear driving my body image behaviors. Show me any behaviors I engage in that separate me from You. In Jesus' name, amen.

Use the space provided to write your own prayer.

Pause to Process

1. Make a list of body behaviors you engage in. Examples can include exercise, nutrition, sleep, or anything else the Lord brings to mind.

_____

_____

_____

_____

_____

_____

2. Circle the behaviors that produce fruit in your life. Those are your faith behaviors.

3. Cross out any behaviors that feel heavy or draining. Those are your fear-driven behaviors. When you feel tempted to slip back into these fear-driven behaviors, stand on the Word of God as your solid foundation. (See the Strong Foundation Verses for ideas.)

Strong Foundation Verses

Use the following scriptural truths to strengthen your foundation. Consider saying them aloud, taking a picture of them to reference, or writing one that stands out on a sticky note and putting it somewhere you will see it daily.

- "Fear of man will prove to be a snare." (Prov. 29:25)
- Be strong and courageous, for the Lord is with you. (Josh. 1:9)
- God has not given you a spirit of fear or timidity. (2 Tim. 1:7)
- "Perfect love drives out fear." (1 John 4:18)
- "[We] will delight in the fear of the LORD." (Isa. 11:2–3)
- Do not fear, for He is our God. (Isa. 41:10)

Let's Rest in God's Word

As you complete this chapter's therapeutic coloring activity, meditate on the key verse and thank God for your body—exactly as it is today.

FOR WE LIVE BY FAITH, NOT BY SIGHT

2 CORINTHIANS 5:7

Unit 3 Counselor's Cornerstone

Strengthening Your Foundation

Let's go deeper into taking our thoughts captive and making them obedient to Christ.

Write Psalm 13:2 in the space provided. Can you relate to wrestling with thoughts about your body image? Use this space to express any frustrations with your thoughts.

Write Psalm 139:23 in the space provided. Use this verse as a prayer to ask the Lord to search your thoughts. We will use one of these thoughts in this unit's Therapy Toolbox.

Write Hebrews 3:1 in the space provided. Do you have trouble fixing your body image thoughts on Jesus? Tell Him about it. He is a safe place to process all your thoughts.

Counselor's Chat

In the unit 3 video, I'm speaking life over your thoughts and emotions. I will walk you through the worksheet to put your thoughts on trial and conclude with a powerful prayer of covering. You can access the video with the QR code on page 22.

Use this triangle to recognize the link between your thoughts, feelings, and behaviors.

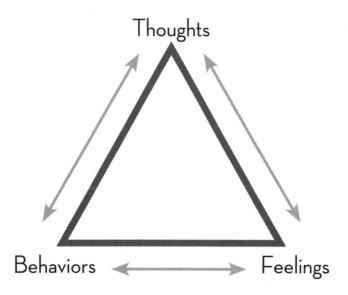

Therapy Toolbox

Remember, our thoughts affect our feelings, and our feelings affect our behaviors. Let's practice putting a thought on trial using a CBT method on the worksheet provided.[2] I have included an example worksheet for reference.

You can use a thought highlighted on your timeline in unit 2 or any others the Lord brings to mind. Keep it simple by challenging only one thought at a time. (You can work through this process with other thoughts in the future.)

1. Write the irrational belief or thought you identified on the How to Put Your Thoughts on Trial worksheet provided.
2. Now defend your thought. Ideally, in a legal trial, evidence can only be used if it's a verifiable fact. No interpretations, guesses, or opinions are allowed.

3. Next, prosecute your thought by writing evidence against it.

4. It's time for the judge to make the decision about this thought. With God as the judge, what would He say to you? Remember, His voice is one of love, not shame.

5. Search God's Word for truth to replace that lie. Consider using a Bible app to search for verses that apply to your thought that you put on trial.

HOW TO PUT YOUR THOUGHTS ON TRIAL

THE THOUGHT:

DEFENSE: PROSECUTION:

EVIDENCE DEFENDING   EVIDENCE AGAINST
THE THOUGHT   THE THOUGHT

THE JUDGE'S VERDICT:

IS THE THOUGHT ACCURATE AND FAIR?

Unit 4

The Interior

Chapter 10

Decorating with Idols

This is the point in our journey when we take responsibility for the role we play in our body image battle. It's easy to point fingers at others and blame them for our struggles. Though, don't forget: they aren't the enemy. The real enemy of our souls is Satan.

We've seen how culture, family, life experiences, and spoken words shape how we view ourselves, especially our bodies. And every single one of those pieces matters and needs to be addressed. However, we would be missing a huge piece to this puzzle if we bypassed the role of idols in our hearts. While an idol has been known to be a physical god (like the golden calves in the Bible), in today's culture, idolatry comes more in the form of extreme attachment or devotion to something other than God.

When I first started to speak on body image, the core message the Lord gave me was about what happens to the temple when idols enter. I'm going to share that with you in this chapter's Temple Truths, but know this: it may offend you. This message offended me when God first revealed it, and I've seen it offend others as I've shared it in teachings. The offense was so apparent that I could look at the listeners and see two different themes on women's faces—pride or shame. The Lord instructed me to pray over both of those things at the beginning of every message, and I'm going to do the same today before we dive into the deep waters of exposing idols:

> *Father, I speak life over this message You are about to deliver to us about idols*
> *in our hearts. I rebuke the spirits of pride and shame. They must flee in Jesus'*
> *name. Show us hidden idols in our hearts in this area of body image.*

When it comes to body image and idols, most women live in either the land of obsession or the land of neglect. Both lands have different, yet accepted, forms of idols. I spent years swinging back and forth between the two lands. We call this "yo-yo dieting" in the fitness industry. I call it idol swapping, trading one type of idol for another and never addressing the root of the issue. We exchange our love of food for the love of a "perfect" body. Both camps have either a spirit of shame or a spirit of pride attached, but one seems more prominent in each.

The land of neglect is one I lived in when I was younger, before I lost a bunch of weight in high school, as well as on and off throughout my adult years. This land carries a lot of shame and hiding. The idols in this land often express themselves in food, binge eating, hiding, numbing, and various forms of gluttony.

In this land of neglect, pride manifests itself in extreme statements that use words such as "always" and "never." It sometimes comes across as judgment of others who obsess. While pride may seem boastful, shame is the loudest bully in this land of neglect. Shame screams, *"What is wrong with you? Why can't you get yourself together? You will always be fat. Just give up."*

I'm thankful to no longer abide in the land of neglect, but the land of obsession is one I still have to fight to stay out of. If I had written this book five years ago, I would have been writing from that land of obsession, and I'm so grateful the Lord didn't allow me to do that. Idols in this land often look like excessive exercise, exorbitant amounts of money spent on beauty products, constant body checking, daily weighing, and any other obsessive body-related behaviors.

Pride is the bully in this land as it whispers, *"There's nothing wrong with this behavior. Everyone is doing it. You aren't strong or confident unless you care this much about how you look."* Shame also creeps into this land with one bite of a cookie, a day without exercise, or worrying about the calories in a tiny piece of communion bread. Shame bullies the people of this land to keep pushing harder. There is no space for rest in this land of obsession.

Therapist Thoughts

Shame is often associated with "should" statements. This is one type of distorted thinking that affects our decisions. These "shoulds" can often lead us to the land of neglect or obsession when not addressed. Try replacing "I should" with "I get to."

I think most of us have spent at least a little time in both of these lands. I've lived in both, and each time, I could always find a group of people who helped justify my irrational behaviors.

When I lived in the land of neglect, I found friends who would be gluttonous with me, obsessing over our next meal together as if it were our full-time job. When I lived in the land of obsession, I found workout buddies who would praise me for pushing my body to extreme places with no rest and little food.

My concern with some body positivity movements is that we haven't uprooted the idols. We've only replaced them with different ones.

So how do you know if you have an idol in this area of body image? A statement attributed to Timothy Keller sums it up best: "Idols consume you as you pursue them, disappoint you when you get them, and devastate you when you lose them."

Let's break that down in practical terms.

> **Idols *consume* you.** When I live in the land of neglect, I am consumed by food. I dream about it. My thoughts focus on what dessert I should make or where I should order takeout.
>
> When I live in the land of obsession, I am consumed by the latest diet trend or exercise program. I submerge myself in researching the latest and greatest beauty products to erase my wrinkles or cellulite.
>
> Take a quick inventory of what is currently consuming your thoughts, time, money, and energy. The chances are high that you will find an idol hiding in there. For as Matthew 6:21 reminds us, "Where your treasure is, there your heart will be also."

> **Idols *disappoint* you.** Five years ago, when I was living in that land of obsession, I finally reached my goal weight. My stomach was the flattest it had been since before I'd given birth to my children. My arms and legs were toned, and I had a beautiful tan. I remember looking in the mirror and thinking, *Hmm, I finally like my body.* Ironically, my very next thought was: *This wasn't what I expected.*

Many of us live under this assumption that when we finally get the body we've always wanted or are making the kind of money we've always dreamed of, *then* we will be happy. But the truth is that if we weren't satisfied without it, we definitely won't be fulfilled with it. There are few things as disappointing as arriving at the top of the mountain and realizing the view isn't at all what we thought it would be.

That's precisely what happens with our pursuit of idols. When we finally get what we have been striving for, those idols disappoint us, as we realize they will never fill a hole in our souls that only God can fill.

Idols *devastate* you. God does not bless our idols. In fact, He gives us strict orders in the Ten Commandments not to worship idols. Thus, anything that is not from God will always leave us feeling empty and devastated. If you've ever lost weight only to gain it all back and then some, you know the depths of this sinking feeling.

God is the only one worthy of consuming our hearts. He will never disappoint us. My father often says, "God is never the source of our disappointment." We will not be devastated by Him because He will never leave or forsake us, though the Enemy might try to convince us otherwise.

> When we finally get what we have been striving for, those idols disappoint us, as we realize they will never fill a hole in our souls that only God can fill.

Where do we reside, then, if we aren't to live in the land of neglect or obsession? Our goal is to live in the land of peace that can only be found in Jesus. Exercise and eating whole foods are both healthy behaviors when submitted to Jesus. Resting and enjoying sweets and other comfort foods in moderation can be a blessing when submitted to the Lord. It is not our job to be the idol police to others; that's the job of the Holy Spirit. What looks restricting or obsessive to one might be entirely different for another. Only the Lord knows the human heart. Let Him be the Holy Spirit to you, your family, and your friends as He reveals the sneaky idols in our hearts.

Temple Truths

I'm not gifted at interior design. I always appreciate when someone has the gift of making a home look beautiful and feel cozy. Decorations in a home tell a story and often reflect the personality of an individual or family. I see this same theme in church buildings.

In fact, I was walking into a church the first time God began to reveal my body image idols. The church was naturally beautiful, and it happened to be decorated for a women's conference. I gasped several times as I saw breathtaking decorations in every corner, each unique and beautiful in its own way. As I admired the beauty of that church, I felt God impress upon my heart, *"Rachael, it's beautiful, isn't it? But did you come to worship the building or Me?"*

I knew exactly what God was saying at that moment. While God loves for church buildings to be beautiful, He never intended for us to be more impressed with the man-made structure than with the Creator. It would be insanity to walk into a church building and bow down to worship the building. It would also be out of order to vandalize a church building, sticking gum on the pews and spraying graffiti on the walls.

Remember in chapter 2 when we discussed how we are God's mobile temples? We should honor our bodies. But just as we would neither bow to worship a church building nor mistreat it, we should avoid worshipping or mistreating our bodies. Your body is a temple to be taken care of, not an idol to be worshipped.

The Bible is clear about how much God detests idols. The Hebrew word for "idol" is *atsab* and means "a formed and fashioned object believed by its maker to contain or represent a deity, and so an object of worship and reverence."[1] Many of the 205 references to the word *idol* are found in the Old Testament, where God continually told His people not to worship idols. If we follow the stories closely, we see that a people or kingdom fell when idols entered.

Second Corinthians 6:16 sums up what happens when idols enter: "What agreement is there between the temple of God and idols? For we are the temple of the living God. As God has said: 'I will live with them and walk among them, and I will be their God, and they will be my people.'"

All God has ever wanted was to walk among His people and be our God. Here are a few powerful verses that reflect how God feels about idols:

- "Do not turn to idols or make metal gods for yourselves. I am the LORD your God." (Lev. 19:4)
- "Watch yourselves very carefully, so that you do not become corrupt and make for yourselves an idol, an image of any shape, whether formed like a man or a woman." (Deut. 4:15–16)
- "Cursed is anyone who makes an idol—a thing detestable to the LORD, the work of skilled hands—and sets it up in secret." (Deut. 27:15)
- "They made him jealous with their foreign gods and angered him with their detestable idols." (Deut. 32:16)

God detests anything that comes between Him and us. The temple falls when idols enter because we turn our hearts away from the Lord and worship a god that can never meet our deepest needs.

It's tempting to skim the chapters in the Old Testament that talk about idols because we think that topic doesn't apply to us. While we may not build golden images to worship today, we have many modern-day idols. Our lust for the perfect body is the modern-day version of the golden idols carved by the Israelites. We see people become famous online simply by posting selfies that display their chiseled bodies. We applaud each other for spending hours creating the body we have always dreamed of having. Yet so few of us applaud each other for obedience to the Lord in our everyday lives behind closed doors. Let's be honest; if our spirits were easily visible to others, we would take better care of them. We obsess over the body because it's what people see, but God looks at the heart (see 1 Sam. 16:7).

This temptation to turn to idols began with Eve in Genesis 3:6: "When the woman saw that the fruit of the tree was good for food and pleasing to the eye, and also desirable for gaining wisdom, she took some and ate it." Eve got distracted by the idol of wisdom, or power, rather than choosing obedience to the Lord. She gave in to that temptation, and we've been battling idols ever since.

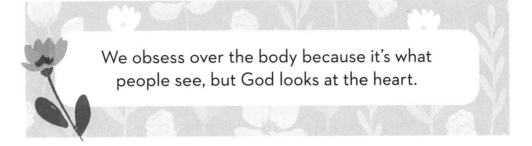

We obsess over the body because it's what people see, but God looks at the heart.

Here's the good news: God knew He would battle against idols to keep our hearts turned toward Him. It's not a surprise to Him. This is just one more reason He sent Jesus to die for our sins. The answer to overcoming idols is letting Jesus access every area of our hearts.

Demolishing idols in our hearts is quite easy, but it requires obedience. Jeremiah 4:1–2 gives us specific instructions,

> "If you, Israel, will return,
>   then return to me,"
>   declares the LORD.
> "If you put your detestable idols out of my sight
>   and no longer go astray,
> and if in a truthful, just and righteous way
>   you swear, 'As surely as the LORD lives,'
> then the nations will invoke blessings by him
>   and in him they will boast."

All we have to do is confess our sins and *return to Him*. We just spent an entire chapter bringing awareness to our body image idols. Let's repent and return to the Lord.

Body Image Blueprint

Now it's time to pray, process, and praise through what we just learned.

Let's Pray

Father, I confess I have idols in this area of body image. [Repent for anything specific the Lord brings to mind.] I choose to demolish those idols in my heart, and I return to You, my first love. I receive Your forgiveness and blessing. Show me the way I should go. To You I entrust my life. In Jesus' name, amen.

Use the space provided to write your own prayer.

Pause to Process

1. What idols do you have in this area of body image? Be honest with yourself and God. Remember, God brings conviction, not condemnation. No shame allowed!

_____

_____

_____

_____

_____

_____

_____

_____

_____

_____

2. If we look closely at our idols, they often reveal what's missing in our hearts. Now that you've identified an idol in this area of body image, ask your soul what hole it's trying to fill. Write your reflections here.

_____

_____

_____

_____

_____

_____

_____

Strong Foundation Verses

Use the following scriptural truths to strengthen your foundation. Consider saying them aloud, taking a picture of them to reference, or writing one that stands out on a sticky note and putting it somewhere you will see it daily.

- There is no agreement between the temple of God and idols. (2 Cor. 6:16)
- "Do not turn to idols." (Lev. 19:4)
- Watch yourself carefully that you don't become corrupt and make an idol for yourself. (Deut. 4:15–16)
- "Cursed is anyone who makes idol … and sets it up in secret." (Deut. 27:15)
- "Flee from idolatry." (1 Cor. 10:14)
- "Dear children, keep yourselves from idols." (1 John 5:21)
- "Those who cling to worthless idols turn away from God's love for them." (Jon. 2:8)

Let's Rest in God's Word

As you complete this chapter's therapeutic coloring activity, meditate on the key verse and thank God for your body—exactly as it is today.

DEAR CHILDREN, KEEP YOURSELVES FROM IDOLS.

DEAR CHILDREN, KEEP YOURSELVES FROM IDOLS.

1 JOHN 5:21

Chapter 11

The House Next Door

From the corner lot where our home is situated, our kitchen sink faces the road. Our neighbors love to decorate their yard every holiday, and many days as we wash dishes, we enjoy seeing what they are putting up in their yard. The day after Halloween, they were creating a magical Christmas tree farm. We happened to be in the market for a Christmas tree, so Matt joked that I could go shopping for one in their pretend lot.

While we admire our neighbors' decor, I can't help but look over to our house and see nothing but a small tree and doormat on the front entrance. For a moment, I am tempted to run out and buy all the things to make our lawn beautiful like theirs. But I would be taking action strictly from a place of comparison and envy, not because I wanted to take the time and money to decorate our yard. (As I said before, decorating is not my natural talent.)

This struggle with comparison and envy runs wide and deep. Comparison is no respecter of age, race, demographics, or religion. It started in the garden, and it continues through all circles of our lives today, even in the church.

Andy Stanley describes the problem with jealousy in his book *Enemies of the Heart*:

> Jealousy is dangerous. It's dangerous because it shapes our attitudes toward other people. It's hard to actively love someone you're jealous of. It's hard to serve (or submit to) someone who's a constant reminder of what you're not. Eventually, jealousy takes control of our attitudes

toward people who have done nothing more than pull ahead of us in a race they're not even aware of.[1]

When it comes to body image, I've rarely compared myself with women built differently from me. When I stand up straight, I'm five foot four, so I've never compared myself to my tall friends. In my mind, that would have been like comparing apples to oranges. No matter what I did, I knew I could never hustle enough to grow taller, so trying to look like them wasn't a temptation.

I did, however, compare myself to a high school friend who was built exactly like me. We were the same height and shape, and even looked like sisters. If one of us lost five pounds, the other was sure to follow. Eventually, my friend and I parted ways, and I never really understood why. Now I see it was because our friendship was built on an unhealthy foundation of comparison and envy. I call this type of unspoken communication in a relationship "yardsticking." It's as though we are walking around with a yardstick in hand, measuring ourselves against others. Of course, this type of comparison is harmful in many ways.

First, comparison robs us of joy. When we are busy looking over, comparing ourselves to others, we fail to see who God created us to be. Nothing steals more joy than to lose sight of ourselves in comparison to someone else.

Next, comparison steals our peace. Just as I was motivated to decorate by looking at my neighbor's lawn, we may feel inspired to succeed by seeing the success of others. Ecclesiastes 4:4 sums this up perfectly; "Then I observed that most people are motivated to success because they envy their neighbors. But this, too, is meaningless—like chasing the wind" (NLT). To spend time comparing is likened to chasing the wind. We go nowhere, and we end up exhausted.

> When we are busy looking over, comparing ourselves to others, we fail to see who God created us to be.

Finally, comparison puts a barrier between us and others. If you've ever had a friendship end and you didn't know why, or you just can't seem to get close to certain people, it might be due to your imaginary yardstick (or theirs). In the case of my friend whose body I often compared mine to, when I tried to enter into a relationship, that yardstick was preventing us from getting close. That yardstick had words such as *jealousy, pride, shame*, and *insecurity* written all over it. If I ever wanted to go deeper with that friend, that stick had to be broken.

While that friend is no longer in my life, I've learned to demolish yardsticks of comparison when I feel them dividing relationships. I've come up with three simple action steps to break down comparison yardsticks.

How to Break Down a Comparison Yardstick

- **Recognize:** In counseling, bringing things to awareness is the first step to healing. If we aren't aware we are using the comparison yardstick, then we can't remove it. First, ask God to show you any comparison traps you've fallen into with others, especially in this area of comparing your body to other women's.
- **Repent:** Ask both God and your friend or family member for forgiveness. I once did this with a friend I only knew online, and while it was an awkward conversation, our relationship deepened, and I was able to be genuinely happy for her. Isn't it incredible how the chains fall off when we bring things into the light?
- **Rejoice:** There is nothing that brings comparison crashing down quicker than using our mouths to thank God for how He made the person you were comparing yourself to. This act of obedience releases pride and restores our joy while blessing our friends.

My friends, if you struggle with comparison, you are not alone. In fact, I have yet to meet someone who doesn't struggle in this area. I have, however, learned how to recognize it quickly so it doesn't have a stronghold in my life.

Let's take that *recognize* bullet point from above a step further and identify a few sneaky signs of comparison that often go undetected.

Signs You Might Struggle with Body Comparison

- You body-check yourself against others.
- You are motivated to change your appearance by looking at photos of fitness models or friends.
- You have a hard time getting close in relationships due to jealousy and insecurity.
- You compare yourself to a younger version of yourself.
- You feel bitterness in your heart toward others and are tempted to gossip about them.
- You have an unhealthy idea of your ideal weight or clothing size.

Comparison comes for all of us, so let's be prepared when it knocks on the door.

Therapist Thoughts

Body-checking is the habit of seeking (or avoiding) information about your body's weight, shape, size, or appearance. It's normal to look in the mirror to make sure you don't have spinach stuck in your teeth or to admire a new outfit. A counselor can help if body-checking becomes problematic or interferes with your life, affects your eating habits, or becomes a way to control fear and anxiety about your body. When you find yourself body-checking, take a moment to check in with your heart and ask, *What am I looking for?*

Temple Truths

Not only does comparison bring division between us and others, but it also separates us from God. I once heard Pastor Robert Morris describe the sin of comparison this way, "There are only two options when we compare: we either puff ourselves up with pride because we find we are better than the other person, or we clothe ourselves in shame because we discover we are inferior."

The result of comparison is always death and destruction. We see comparison first creep into the garden when Satan tempted Eve (see Gen. 3:2–6). I call this encounter the first before and after in the Bible.

Satan had already "fallen" by comparing himself to God, and now he was on a mission to bring humankind down with him. He painted a before and after for Eve to make her crave what she didn't have. In that brief moment, Eve forgot she already had everything she ever needed, and she allowed comparison to cause her to act out of character. Eve was lured in by the beauty of the food and the promise of wisdom to come. The apple didn't fall far from the tree as we watch comparison and jealousy tear Eve's sons, Cain and Abel, apart (see Gen. 4:1–16).

Here are a few more times we see the spirit of comparison and jealousy wreak havoc in the Bible:

- Jacob and Esau (Gen. 25; 27)
- Leah and Rachel (Gen. 29–30)
- Joseph and his brothers (Gen. 37)
- Saul and David (1 Sam. 15–31)

This body image battle we face today has the same roots we see in the garden and throughout the Bible: a desire for more beauty, wisdom, and power than we were given. Perhaps this is why James 3:16 warns us, "For where you have envy and selfish ambition, there you find disorder and every evil practice."

If you've ever wondered where God stands on this topic of comparison and envy, that verse is as straightforward as it gets. He hates envy and comparison because of the disorder and chaos they release in our lives. Notice I said God hates envy; I did not say He hates the envious person or the person being envied.

In previous chapters, we saw in Genesis 3:7—immediately after Satan painted the before and after for Eve—that shame entered the scene. The bait of comparison opened the door for shame. Eve is not alone in taking the bait of comparison. Every time I take the bait, it ends in shame or another prideful spirit that separates me from God.

Here comes a full-circle moment that blew me away when I discovered it. We know this body image battle started in the garden and ended on the cross. But did you realize that both Eve and Jesus wrestled with temptation in a garden? Eve's garden moment ended in sin and shame. Jesus' garden moment ended in the defeat of the Enemy and in victory. Eve symbolizes all of humanity in our human limitations. Eve is not a lone ranger who made a mistake and ruined it for all of us. If you or I had been in that garden, chances are high we would have made the same mistake because we are sinners in need of the Savior.

Let's read the story of Jesus in the garden of Gethsemane, in Matthew 26:36–42. (I highly recommend taking the time to read the entire chapter.)

> Then Jesus came with them to a place called Gethsemane, and told His disciples, "Sit here while I go over there and pray...." Then He said to them, "My soul is deeply grieved, to the point of death; remain here and keep watch with Me."
>
> And He went a little beyond them, and fell on His face and prayed, saying, "My Father, if it is possible, let this cup pass from Me; yet not as I will, but as You will." And He came to the disciples and found them sleeping, and He said to Peter, "So, you men could not keep watch with Me for one hour? Keep watching and praying, so that you do not come into temptation; the spirit is willing, but the flesh is weak."
>
> He went away again a second time and prayed, saying, "My Father, if this cup cannot pass away unless I drink from it, Your will be done."
> (NASB)

Jesus knew the Enemy's character was to thwart the plans of God. He had already succeeded in the garden with Eve, but Jesus was prepared for the temptation that was to come His way. Jesus' victory on the cross started by resisting the Enemy in the garden. That victory is the only thing that can empower us to resist the temptation to give space to envy and comparison in our lives. If we rely solely on our own strength, we may never stop comparing our bodies to others, but through Christ all things are possible.

Body image comparison is a trap that weighs many women down. Hebrews 12:1–2 gives us this bold reminder: "Therefore, since we are surrounded by such a great cloud of witnesses, let us throw off everything that hinders and the sin that so easily entangles. And let us run with perseverance the race marked out for us, fixing our eyes on Jesus, the pioneer and perfecter of faith." We are called to throw off everything that hinders and holds us back, including body comparison.

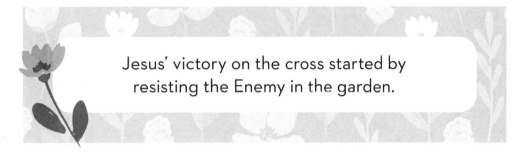

Jesus' victory on the cross started by resisting the Enemy in the garden.

I leave you with one final charge on this comparison topic that comes from 1 Corinthians 3:3–17.

First, we see this topic of jealousy come up in verse 3, "For since there is jealousy and quarreling among you, are you not worldly? Are you not acting like mere humans?"

Next, we see the topic of comparison concerning who the people think is the best to follow: "For when one says, 'I follow Paul,' and another, 'I follow Apollos,' are you not mere human beings? What, after all, is Apollos? And what is Paul? Only servants, through whom you came to believe—as the Lord has assigned to each his task" (vv. 4–5).

Then the passage goes on to say that each one of them played a role that is no greater than the other's. "I planted the seed, Apollos watered it, but God has been making it grow. So neither the one who plants nor the one who waters is anything, but only God, who makes things grow" (vv. 6–7).

In verses 9–11, we see this full-circle moment where we are reminded of our purpose and upon whom our foundation should be built: "For we are co-workers in God's service; you are God's field, God's building. By the grace God has given me, I laid a foundation as a wise builder, and someone else is building on it. But each one should build with care. For no one can lay any foundation other than the one already laid, which is Jesus Christ."

And finally, in verses 16–17, we are reminded of the original design for our bodies: "Don't you know that you yourselves are God's temple and that God's Spirit dwells in your midst? If anyone destroys God's temple, God will destroy that person; for God's temple is sacred, and you together are that temple."

What if the destruction of our temples is coming in the form of comparison? Let's take action today to kick comparison to the curb through the power of Christ within our temples.

Body Image Blueprint

Now it's time to pray, process, and praise through what we just learned.

Let's Pray

Father, thank You that You designed my body to be a temple where You could reside. Thank You for loving me too much to let comparison be a stumbling block. Show me the areas where I fall into the temptation to compare. I repent for the envy and jealousy in my heart. May the joy of the Lord be my strength as I stand up to comparison. In Jesus' name, amen.

Use the space provided to write your own prayer.

Pause to Process

1. Who have you compared your body to?

_____

_____

_____

_____

_____

_____

2. What did you lose by the comparison?

_____

_____

_____

_____

_____

_____

_____

_____

_____

_____

Strong Foundation Verses

Use the following scriptural truths to strengthen your foundation. Consider saying them aloud, taking a picture of them to reference, or writing one that stands out on a sticky note and putting it somewhere you will see it daily.

- When we measure and compare ourselves by ourselves, we are not wise. (2 Cor. 10:12)
- "Where you have envy and selfish ambition, there you find disorder." (James 3:16)
- "Who … can compare with the LORD?" (Ps. 89:6 NLT)
- Take pride in yourself alone, without comparing to someone else. (Gal. 6:4)
- "There is jealousy and quarreling among you." (1 Cor. 3:3)

Let's Rest in God's Word

As you complete this chapter's therapeutic coloring activity, meditate on the key verse and thank God for your body—exactly as it is today.

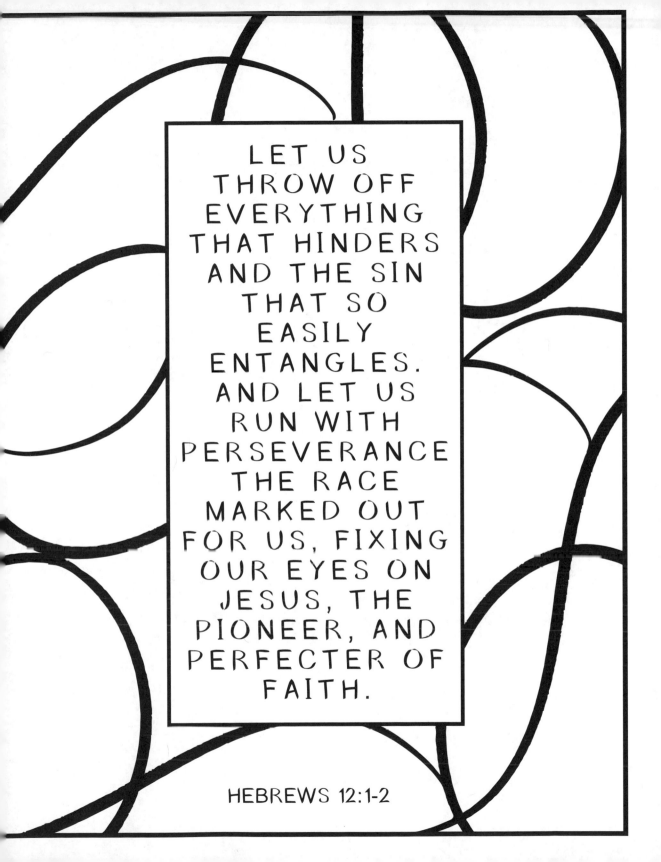

LET US THROW OFF EVERYTHING THAT HINDERS AND THE SIN THAT SO EASILY ENTANGLES. AND LET US RUN WITH PERSEVERANCE THE RACE MARKED OUT FOR US, FIXING OUR EYES ON JESUS, THE PIONEER, AND PERFECTER OF FAITH.

HEBREWS 12:1-2

Chapter 12

Moldy Motives

A few years ago, my family returned from a lovely weekend getaway of fun and relaxation. When we opened the door to our home, we were hit with a smell so strong, we suspected we'd either forgotten to take out the trash or an animal had found its way into our home and met its demise. Either of those options would have been better than what we discovered in our master bedroom closet. We rounded the corner to see water pouring down through a hole in the ceiling. Our clothes and carpet were drenched. We ran upstairs to find our daughter's bathroom sink overflowing with water. We'd soon learn that our air conditioner had become clogged, causing water to flow out from her sink.

The result? A flooded upstairs bathroom, bedrooms, hall, and of course, our downstairs closet. We did our best to clean things with towels and the fans we owned, but the next day, the demolition crew came to do the deep work. They ripped up the carpet and knocked bigger holes in the walls to help things dry out before putting it all back together. The fans they brought in were the huge, high-powered ones that you can hear from a mile away. I was ready for them to patch things up immediately, but instead, they assured us we had to leave the fans on until the structures were completely dry. If we rushed this process, we could end up with mold growth.

Those fans ran twenty-four hours a day in our house for two weeks. *Two weeks.* It sounds like a short amount of time now, but while living in the home, it felt like it would never end. We were homeschooling at the time, and we couldn't hear each other speak. We would frequently slip away to the library to give our brains a break.

One night as I lay in bed, trying to fall asleep amid the chaos, I begged my husband, "Can we please just start the rebuilding?! This is making me crazy!"

> God brings things up because they are on the way out.

As much as Matt was also over it, we'd both read enough stories of people becoming chronically ill from mold in their walls. My impatient flesh was begging for a shortcut around the problem, while my spirit knew we needed to wait and do things correctly.

Eventually, the fans were removed and construction was underway. It took about six months to put our home back in order, and in that time, I learned many important lessons about patience and endurance.

This morning, as I sat and had my quiet time in that same closet that had been under construction for months, the Lord reminded me why it is crucial to give the healing process time. If we try to rush things, we may end up with mold in the walls of our hearts.

Throughout this book, we have uncovered some painful issues that you may have been avoiding for a long time. We've tapped wounds and hidden sin you may not have even realized you still carried. The Lord spotlights these "moldy" parts of our hearts for a reason. But it's important to be patient while He reveals our wounds and heals them.

Just last week, the Lord revealed some hidden mold in my heart around this topic of body image. Matt and I were invited to help with a fitness project for a marriage ministry. Even though I had taught fitness for more than a decade, I had taken the last few years off to complete graduate school. I did my best to teach these videos, but I was not prepared for the emotions that would surface when we arrived on set.

As I wrangled my way into my leggings and the tank top that had been provided, I looked down to see my muffin top hanging over the edge of my pants. The first thought that came to mind was, *Oh my goodness, what am I doing here?! I don't look the part of the fitness instructor. They should have asked someone else to do this.* Thankfully, I have come to recognize the Enemy's voice quickly in this area and rebuked that thought as soon as it surfaced. But I was surprised to discover that old belief was still there, hidden in the walls of my heart.

Remember the story I shared in a previous chapter about the fitness instructor who loved my skill but told me I needed to work on my appearance? While it's true the Enemy used that instructor to get me to believe that if I didn't look the part, then I couldn't play the role, there was more going on in my heart I didn't yet see. Even though I had replaced his lie with biblical truth all those years ago, I had never properly dealt with that mold. Instead, I'd simply walled off that part of my heart and avoided dealing with the core belief until it all resurfaced recently, forcing me to dig deep as I stared down at my muffin top, asking God for confidence to show up on set.

I finally confronted this hard truth: I wanted to look good on set because of my pride, not for God's glory. Beneath that pride was a false belief that I had to earn my worth.

These negative core beliefs are what I refer to as moldy motives in the walls of our hearts. If we don't take time to deal with them when they arise, our hearts will carry a toxic poison that will wreak havoc in our lives. This mold I was carrying about my worth equaling my appearance almost disqualified me from showing up fully where God had planted me. My pride and per-fectionist spirit tried to bench me. Thankfully, Jesus and His grace swooped in to save the day.

Therapist Thoughts

People are not born with core beliefs; they are learned. What core beliefs have you learned about your body that God would love to rewrite?

My friend, if you are ready to throw in the towel on doing this deep work, you are not alone. This is not an easy journey. I am so proud of you for continuing to show up and take this walk with me. One of my graduate school professors, Dr. Linda Hoover, once said, "God brings things up because they are on the way out." If difficult issues are coming up for you now, that is good news because they are on the way out. Let them come up so God can heal and restore this destructive area of your life.

Temple Truths

Did you know that the Bible has something to say about dealing with mold in walls? In Leviticus 14:33–57, God gives specific instructions on what a priest was to do if mold was found in a home. While I encourage you to read all twenty-five verses on your own, I want to highlight some key takeaways from this passage of Scripture:

- *There will be mold.* The Lord didn't say *if* mold appears when He gave the priests instructions on how to uproot the mold. Instead, He said *when* mold appears. We all have mold growing in our hearts. It's up to us to allow the Lord to reveal and heal it.
- *We have a plan to get rid of the mold.* Just as the Lord gave the priests specific instructions on how to cleanse the house of mold, He has given us Jesus to consecrate our hearts daily so that the mold doesn't return.
- *The Lord is not done with the house.* Much like when my home was threatened by mold, I wondered, as I read these passages on mold removal, why they didn't just knock the structure down and start over. God is in the business of restoration both in the seen and the unseen. No matter your age, it is never too late to rebuild your view of body image and get rid of the mold plaguing your heart.

Why does God care about getting rid of the mold in our hearts in this area of body image? For many reasons, one of which is to help us take our place as defenders of life. Let's go back to the first woman created, Eve, to explore some significant themes about her design.

The name Eve is an archaic form of *haya*, meaning "living thing."[1] In Genesis 2:21–22, we learn that Eve was formed from one rib of Adam, "So the LORD God caused the man to fall into a deep sleep; and while he was sleeping, he took one of the man's ribs and then closed up the place with flesh. Then the LORD God made a woman from the rib he had taken out of the man, and he brought her to the man."

It is ironic to consider Eve came from a rib and now we live in a culture that glorifies being able to see a woman's ribs. I spy the Enemy twisting something else God intended for good.

Eve being formed from a rib is symbolic in that the primary function of ribs is to protect vital organs and aid in breathing. When Matt and I took human anatomy in college, we saw with our own eyes how the ribs protect the vital organs. Without ribs, our organs would suffer harm from external threats. While it hurts to break a rib, it is better than a pierced organ, which could lead to death.

All women, whether they have biological children or not, are defenders of life. As women in the body of Christ, we serve as "ribs" defending against the attacks of the Enemy on the "internal organs" of the body. This body image war on women is far more profound than the wrestling within ourselves. This war is attacking our position as defenders of the unseen. The Enemy knows that if he can keep some hidden mold in our hearts, we will shrink back and refuse to take our place in the battle.

God has strategically planted you exactly where you are to defend your territory. As you continue to show up and allow God to reveal and heal the mold in your heart, you will experience a supernatural overflow of energy and life in everything you do. The time is now to stand your ground and defend the vital organs in your life. Your only job is to keep showing up; let God do the heavy lifting in this battle He has already won.

> As you continue to show up and allow God to reveal and heal the mold in your heart, you will experience a supernatural overflow of energy and life in everything you do.

Body Image Blueprint

Now it's time to pray, process, and praise through what we just learned.

Let's Pray

Father, thank You for loving me too much to let me live with mold in my heart. Please reveal any hidden mold that is toxic in my heart and life. Replace that mold with Your truth and the peace that surpasses all understanding. Guard my heart and mind in Christ Jesus. Amen.

Use the space provided to write your own prayer.

Pause to Process

1. One of the best questions I've learned to ask that uproots the mold in my heart is this: "Why are you chasing what you are chasing?" It is essential to clarify *why* we are chasing what we are chasing in the pursuit of the perfect body. Take some time to journal today, and ask God to reveal any *moldy motives* that don't align with His Word.

_____

_____

_____

_____

2. Repent and use the space below to ask God to give you a fresh perspective.

_____

_____

_____

_____

Strong Foundation Verses

Use the following scriptural truths to strengthen your foundation. Consider saying them aloud, taking a picture of them to reference, or writing one that stands out on a sticky note and putting it somewhere you will see it daily.

- Ask the Lord to examine your heart and mind. (Ps. 26:2)
- When the law of God is in your heart, your feet do not slip. (Ps. 37:31)
- Pray for a pure heart and a steadfast spirit. (Ps. 51:10)
- God promises we will be His people when we return to Him. (Jer. 24:7)
- When we seek Him with all our hearts, we will find Him. (Jer. 29:13)
- "Blessed are the pure in heart, for they will see God." (Matt. 5:8)
- "Where your treasure is, there your heart will be also." (Matt. 6:21)

Let's Rest in God's Word

As you complete this chapter's therapeutic coloring activity, meditate on the key verse and thank God for your body—exactly as it is today.

CREATE IN ME A CLEAN HEART, O GOD.
RENEW A LOYAL SPIRIT WITHIN ME.
PSALM 51:10 (NLT)

Unit 4 Counselor's Cornerstone

Strengthening Your Foundation

In this unit, we discussed several things that can cause pain, frustration, and setbacks in our body image healing. One of those areas was idols in our hearts. I know that's the one we would rather not poke at too much, but I want to create space to let the Lord go deeper to reveal anything that is coming between Him and our healing.

Though many verses and stories in the Bible warn against idols, I've hand-selected just a few. I encourage you to take the time to look up the three verses and reflect on what God is saying to you. Grab your Bible and your favorite writing instrument, and let's get to work.

1. **Write Leviticus 19:4.** After you write it, ask the Lord to show you any idols in this area of body image. Be bold and ask Him to show you when these issues surface throughout your day and week.

2. **Read Matthew 4:10.** Did you notice that even Jesus Himself was tempted to bow down to idols? Use the space below to practice using your voice to command Satan to leave in Jesus' name when you are tempted to bow down to anyone or anything that is not God.

_____

_____

_____

_____

_____

_____

_____

_____

_____

3. **Write 1 John 5:21.** I love how this verse begins with "Dear children." It shows God's tender care for His kids. Consider writing this one on a sticky note and putting it in a place where you can be reminded to guard yourself against idols.

_____

_____

_____

_____

_____

_____

_____

_____

Counselor's Chat

In the unit 4 video, I'm speaking life over you in the area of idols, comparison, and motives. I will walk you through the following yardstick activity. You can access the video with the QR code on page 22.

Therapy Toolbox

I introduced the yardstick activity in chapter 11, and now it's your turn to fill it in. Follow these simple steps using the yardstick template.

- Write specific comparisons you make with others. Some examples to get you started might include: body shape, weight, height, complexion, wrinkles, cellulite, giftings, money, house, popularity, spouse, friends, and so on.
- Add names to your yardstick to identify people whose lives you compare to your own. These may be friends, loved ones, coworkers, and others. Remember, this is meant to be your own personal body image diary, but if you feel uncomfortable writing real names, use initials or a name only you would recognize.
- Now that you've associated a comparison with a specific person or group, evaluate your relationship with that person. Do you share a deep and authentic relationship? Or does it feel like something is always between you, keeping you at a distance?
- Strike through each of those comparisons and replace it with what you would like to feel or think about that person, replacing feelings of jealousy, envy, bitterness, resentment, or any other thoughts/emotions that come between you.
- Thank God specifically for this person. Take a moment to pray a blessing over him or her.

YARDSTICKING

Unit 5

The Exterior

Chapter 13

Curb Appeal and Being Real

Our family lives in a neighborhood that is held to rules and standards by a homeowners' association (HOA). If you're not familiar with HOAs, they require residents to receive approval before making any exterior changes to a home or property in the neighborhood. Depending on the specific code restrictions, this may include anything from putting in a new fence or repainting the porch to placing signs or flags in the yard. They also drive through the neighborhood and take photos of anything that looks out of order. If they spot anything, like a dead tree or an uncut lawn, they may mail a letter to let you know you have a certain amount of time to fix the problem or be fined.

We received one of these dreaded letters instructing us to paint our mailbox. Apparently, a faded black mailbox is a big no-no. And we also had to clean up our flower beds and remove a few dead bushes. While we certainly weren't thrilled to get the letter, we knew the HOA was doing an important job to keep the neighborhood looking clean and cohesive.

It would be an oversight to write a book on body image and fail to acknowledge that we live in a world influenced by a "body image HOA." In chapter 1, we discussed how culture shapes our foundational beliefs about our body identity. Now let's come at it from another angle: the expectations we silently put on ourselves from the unspoken messages all around us. While we know that God looks at the heart, our flesh is programmed to look at what meets the eye. This is why this wrestling between caring about external appearance one moment and not caring the next is an ongoing battle in our hearts and minds.

Therapist Thoughts

The brain is far more sophisticated than we realize. No one has to say that we are more valuable, special, or worthy when we are skinny or have a certain body type. Our brains automatically fill in the gaps when we see that those who get the most attention in the media are the thin, youthful, attractive people. This leaves the brain constantly evaluating questions about our identity and worth through the lens of, *How attractive, thin, or acceptable am I?* This is incredibly stressful, as something as important as our worth as human beings is constantly being evaluated based solely on our outward appearance.

On a sticky note, write words of affirmation to retrain your brain to focus on the truth from God's Word. (Adapted from Dr. Shannon Crawford)

I will never forget an HOA body image moment I had to overcome in my marriage as I wrestled between my outward appearance and the beauty of the sacred marriage bed. I had turned down Matt's invitation for sex because I was exhausted from waking up at 4:30 every morning to get to boot camp. On top of predawn boot camp, I was following an extreme diet regimen that left me starving, moody, and burned-out. I hated that I was turning away from my husband, yet at the same time, I felt this odd pressure to continue to get my body into shape. I hit a breaking point and broke down in tears, confessing that I could not keep up the early-morning workouts and dieting. As I poured my heart out, he listened closely and then said, "Rachael, stop comparing yourself to your younger self; she's another woman."

As soon as Matt spoke those words, it was as though the blinders were removed from my eyes. I had been crumbling under the pressure to get back to a version of my fifteen-year-old body. We discussed comparison in chapter 11, but it had never crossed my mind until that day that I'd been comparing myself to my younger self, and even a future version I dreamed of being, not to other women.

The worldview of the body image HOA tells us that if we diet enough, hustle enough, or use enough magic creams, we can look young forever. But our biblical worldview tells us that we are, in fact, designed to age. Our bodies won't perform or look as they did when we were fifteen, and that is okay.

This is not an excuse to neglect our bodies. However, we can spend countless hours and thousands of dollars resisting the natural progression of life, or we can rest in the fact that God created seasons for a reason—seasons of life and seasons for our bodies.

When we compare ourselves to an earlier or different version of ourselves, we miss the blessing of the current season.

When I recognized that I was putting unrealistic expectations on my body, I was able to pause and ask God how to give my body exactly what it needed in that season. I gave up the early-morning boot camp and exchanged it for an 8:00 a.m. workout that was just what my body needed in that challenging season. The fruit that came was more energy, peace, and a renewed love for my body and how far she had brought me. I also found more energy for the things and people I love, like my wise husband.

Let's give our bodies grace to embrace where they are today.

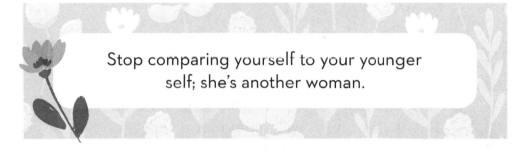

Stop comparing yourself to your younger self; she's another woman.

Temple Truths

This is a great time to return to the foundation that we laid in the beginning and that I've infused throughout this book, which is the Word of God. Proverbs 31:30 tells us that "charm is deceptive, and beauty is fleeting, but a woman who fears the LORD is to be praised." The word *fleeting* in this verse is the Hebrew word *hebel,* meaning "vapor," "breath," "futile," "worthless," or "vain." This is the same word we see in Ecclesiastes 1:2, where the Teacher says, "Everything is meaningless,… completely meaningless!" (NLT)

The author of Ecclesiastes was so passionate about this topic that he mentioned the word *meaningless* thirty-five times in the NIV translation. Essentially, he analyzed the meaning of life and what future generations would remember. He observed that things we toil hard over, like wealth and beauty, are meaningless in the grand scheme of things.

Like money, beauty is a good thing when it comes from God and is used for its intended purpose. Think of the radiant flowers in the field or a golden sunset to ease us into the hours of rest. God created beauty all around for us to enjoy as part of His glorious creation. The problem comes when we worship the beauty of creation over our Creator.

You and I are part of God's creation. Psalm 139:14 says, "I praise you because I am fearfully and wonderfully made; your works are wonderful, I know that full well."

I've heard this verse used often in relation to biblical beauty; however, the first part of praising Him is generally left off. While my beauty may be fleeting, I know that my future grandchildren will not remember Grandma by my wrinkles or gray hair; instead, they will remember a woman who feared and praised the Lord. That is the beauty that carries on for generations to come.

> My future grandchildren will not remember Grandma by my wrinkles or gray hair; instead, they will remember a woman who feared and praised the Lord.

First Samuel 16:7 also contrasts how God sees beauty with how man sees it: "For the LORD sees not as man sees: man looks on the outward appearance, but the LORD looks on the heart" (ESV).

I notice two key points in this verse about outward appearance. First, it confirms that it is natural for humans to look at outward appearance. It's how we are wired. I am not here to shame anyone for noticing outward beauty. As a girl who loves fashion, I will be the first to admit I notice and appreciate an adorable outfit when I see it. I think God loves it when we notice and enjoy the beautiful things in the world around us. It's what makes us human.

The second thing I notice in this verse is that God looks at things from a different perspective than we do. Have you ever had the window seat in an airplane? I love to gaze down on the landscape, as it takes on a completely different look from up above. What once was a vast building now looks like a tiny speck that I could pick up with one hand.

God has this perspective in every area of our lives. What seems enormous and impossible to us is a speck to God. He says in Isaiah 55:8–9, "'For my thoughts are not your thoughts, neither are your ways my ways,' declares the LORD. 'As the heavens are higher than the earth, so are my ways higher than your ways and my thoughts than your thoughts.'"

The second part of 1 Samuel 16:7, about God seeing the heart, is both comforting and awakening. It's comforting to know that no matter what my outward appearance looks like, God looks past it and sees my heart. It's awakening to realize that God sees the areas of my heart that I can't conceal with makeup or cute clothes. He sees my hidden motives, sin, and insecurities and loves me despite it all. While He loves me no matter what, He still wants to help me deal with that hidden junk clogging my heart.

As I've mentioned, my husband, Matt, is a chiropractor, and we own an integrated medical practice. Years ago, when we first started our practice, we would provide workshops in our community to educate people about spinal care. Most individuals fail to take care of their spines because they can't see them. What usually brings them into our clinic is pain.

An analogy we would use to explain preventative health care is a dentist visit. You don't wait until all of your teeth fall out to take care of your teeth, so why would you wait until your spine fails to take care of it? The truth is that if your spine were visible, you would take better care of it. I think this same principle applies to our hearts. If the things that God sees in our hearts were on display for all to see, we would deal with them much quicker. But instead, we place a higher value on what we can see.

Oftentimes, we wait until the pain becomes unbearable before we finally deal with hard truths. But there is a big difference between feeling convicted by the Holy Spirit to bring healing and change and being condemned by the Enemy, which only brings hurt and shame.

God is bringing up this topic not to shame or condemn but to convict and restore. Romans 8:1 says, "There is now no condemnation for those who are in Christ Jesus." Will you be brave with me and allow the Holy Spirit to point out expectations in your heart that need to go?

Body Image Blueprint

Now it's time to pray, process, and praise through what we just learned.

Let's Pray

Father, thank You for making everything beautiful in its time, including me. I know that man looks on outward appearances, but You look at the heart. Please search my heart and show me anything that is not pleasing to You. I repent of the sin that so easily ensnares me. Holy Spirit, I submit my heart to You. May I value the things that matter to You, Lord. Thank You for loving me. I love You. In Jesus' name, amen.

Use the space provided to write your own prayer.

Pause to Process

1. What expectations have you set for yourself about your appearance?

_____

_____

_____

_____

_____

2. What expectations have other people set for your appearance?

_____

_____

_____

_____

_____

_____

_____

_____

_____

_____

_____

_____

3. What does God see when He looks at you?

_____

_____

_____

_____

_____

_____

_____

_____

_____

_____

_____

_____

_____

Strong Foundation Verses

Use the following scriptural truths to strengthen your foundation. Consider saying them aloud, taking a picture of them to reference, or writing one that stands out on a sticky note and putting it somewhere you will see it daily.

- "Charm is deceptive, and beauty is fleeting." (Prov. 31:30)
- "The unfading beauty of a gentle and quiet spirit … is of great worth in God's sight." (1 Pet. 3:4)
- "Outwardly we are wasting away, yet inwardly we are being renewed day by day." (2 Cor. 4:16)
- "The grass withers and the flowers fall, but the word of our God endures forever." (Isa. 40:8)
- "People look at the outward appearance, but the LORD looks at the heart." (1 Sam. 16:7)
- "He has made everything beautiful in its time." (Eccl. 3:11)

Let's Rest in God's Word

As you complete this chapter's therapeutic coloring activity, meditate on the key verse and thank God for your body—exactly as it is today.

CHARM IS DECEPTIVE, AND BEAUTY IS FLEETING; BUT A WOMAN WHO FEARS THE LORD IS TO BE PRAISED.

PROVERBS 31:30

Chapter 14

Break the Alarm Cycle

The first home Matt and I moved into as a young married couple with a newborn baby was adorable, but it happened to be in a sketchy neighborhood. The previous owner had installed a security system with a huge red light embedded in the dining room ceiling. While the light could not be removed without demolishing the ceiling, the real estate agent assured us the siren would only go off if we reactivated the security system.

We'd been living in the home for about a month when, at 2:00 a.m., that red light went off with a vengeance—flashing as brightly as a fire truck, with a siren equally loud. Our newborn woke up, as did Matt (who could typically sleep through a tornado). Certain an intruder was in our home, he lunged out of bed and found the nearest weapon he could find, which happened to be a baseball bat. He scanned the perimeters, sporting nothing but his boxers and the bat. In hindsight, the image of him makes me giggle, but at the time, it was no laughing matter.

Once he determined all was clear, he went to work trying to shut off that deafening and blinding alarm. This took a long time because he had to remove the entire unit from the wall and cut the cords.

Finally, we had silence again in our home. Yet our hearts raced faster than ever.

Thankfully, there had been no intruder, and the chaos had been caused by a glitch in the system. But ever since that day, I've had trust issues with alarm systems. *Are we really in danger, or is it another glitch?*

Of course, this mindset puts me at risk. While we can't over-rely on man-made alarms, as they will sometimes fail us, we do need to react appropriately when they warn us of potential danger.

The same is true of our body's alarm system.

Often, what we see being expressed on the external parts of our bodies reflects what is going on inside. For example, adult acne *can be* a sign of problems with gut health, extra fat around the stomach *can be* a precursor to heart disease, spinal issues *may be* interfering with nerve function, and a headache *can be* a sign of dehydration. (Notice I italicized *can be* and *may be* because these are examples, not medical advice.)

This list could go on, but here's the key takeaway I want you to remember: your body is always speaking to you. Sometimes the things you see expressed on the exterior of your body are evident because your interior body is screaming, *Help me! I'm not okay!*

I encourage you to love your body by listening to her.

Recently, I had an "Aha!" moment about this concept in my own life. For the last three years, I've battled some health symptoms. About a year into graduate school, I noticed I had put on some weight. My jeans were tighter, and the buttons on my tops were threatening to bust wide open. I ignored that alarm system and attributed the weight gain to the fact that I was spending more time sitting.

Therapist Thoughts

Here are three questions to ponder when deciding if weighing is best for you:

1. Do you currently struggle with (or are you at risk of) an eating disorder? People who are in treatment or recovering from an eating disorder are discouraged from weighing daily.

2. What does the number represent for you? If your mood rises or falls based on the number on the scale, it may be time to step away for a season.

3. What is God saying to you about weighing? Trust Him to show you the best way to honor your body.

The next symptom that popped up was acne. Again, it was annoying, but I grabbed some zit cream and called it good.

Then the fatigue set in. It was the kind of fatigue where I would get eight hours of sleep and still wake up feeling exhausted. I justified the fatigue due to an overloaded schedule and assured myself that things would be better once I graduated. I grabbed my extra dose of caffeine and kept moving forward.

As time went on, more and more symptoms appeared—moodiness, irritability, decreased libido, depression, and ultimately, total burnout. When I finally went to the doctor, blood work revealed that I was anemic and had developed hypothyroidism and adrenal fatigue.

While it wasn't the news I wanted to hear, it felt great to have some answers and a plan to help restore my body. You see? The extra weight, acne, and fatigue had actually served as my body's alarm system warning me to slow down and take care of myself. All my attempts at a quick fix could not override my body's way of trying to get back to good health.

The battle was never about the appearance of my body. She just wanted to take care of me so that I could walk fully in my God-given purpose as a mom, wife, friend, author, encourager, and counselor.

This is a chance for us to take a step back and evaluate if your disconnection with your body might be due to you silencing her alarm systems. What if the desire to change how you look is rooted in a desire to take better care of your body? What if it's not about the looks at all?

Temple Truths

When I started the journey of healing from the inflammatory diseases, God taught me how to care for my body in a way that was both honoring to Him and good for my body. Before I introduce those principles, let's address why healthy habits matter.

Healthy habits run much deeper than external appearance. Muscles, for example, are a fruit of our obedience to move. I have muscles in places I don't see them, like my abs, but I still strengthen my core because it is good for my health.

In 1 Corinthians 10:31–33, we see specific instructions: "So whether you eat or drink or whatever you do, do it all for the glory of God. Do not cause anyone to stumble, whether Jews, Greeks or the church of God—even as I try to please everyone in every way. For I am not seeking my own good but the good of many, so that they may be saved."

This charge to be mindful of all we do, from eating and drinking to where we go and what we do, is our motivation to be submitted in this area to God. It's not a matter of hustling or putting on a show to impress others. Instead, it's the realization that both believers and unbelievers observe everything we do. If any of our actions cause others to stumble, we should consider eliminating those habits. Our healthy habits serve God, our bodies, and those around us.

Frequently, our unhealthy habits serve our sinful nature and rarely point people back to God. So how do we determine which habits are healthy and which aren't?

For starters, trust your gut. And we do that with the help of the Holy Spirit.

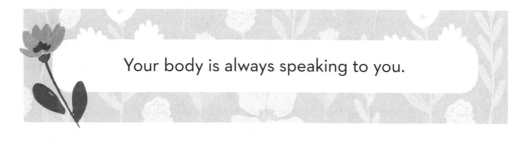

Your body is always speaking to you.

Most of us know when we are engaged in a habit that is not serving God, us, or others. It's tempting to silence the voice of the Holy Spirit because that means we must give up control. But Jesus was clear that the Holy Spirit is our friend. We see this come to life in John 16:7 in *The Message*: "So let me say it again, this truth: It's better for you that I leave. If I don't leave, the Friend won't come. But if I go, I'll send him to you."

How cool that Jesus sent us a Helper to be our Friend who guides us to make wise decisions! Because of the free will God has given us and the freedom we have in Christ, we technically have the right to silence our Friend and do anything that feels good in the moment. Sure, I have the right to eat an entire package of Oreos, which I have been known to do in my disordered-eating days. But is that what my Friend, the Holy Spirit, would have directed me to do? My body and my upset stomach say no. After such an encounter, I find myself with a stomachache, brain fog, irritability, and the urge to take a nap. In that condition, I am no longer able to serve anyone around me.

When the Lord first taught me His way of taking care of my body, He told me, "Submit your heart, renew your mind, and embrace a strong body." Let's take a closer look at these three aspects of the healing process.

Submitted Heart

You may have noticed the theme of the heart repeated many times throughout this book. That's because the Bible has a lot to say about it—762 mentions in the NIV version, to be exact. Often, before someone turned away from God or other people, that person first hardened his own heart (for example, see Ex. 8:15, 32; 2 Chron. 36:13). This is still true today in marriage and other close-knit relationships. This is likely why God tells us in Proverbs 4:23, "Above all else, guard your heart, for everything you do flows from it."

To bring this heart issue back to our bodies, let's look at Proverbs 3:5–6: "Trust in the LORD with all your heart and lean not on your own understanding; in all your ways submit to him, and he will make your paths straight."

The act of submitting our hearts to the Lord daily is the most important healthy habit we can create in this area of body image. Listening to our bodies' alarm system when things are off internally starts with submitting our hearts to the Lord. He will give us peace, wisdom, and direction when we let Him speak into this area.

Sound Mind

We've talked about the power of our thoughts in chapter 7. Let's look at our mindset when it comes to habits.

One thing that every health professional can agree upon is that our bodies need whole foods, especially fiber-rich vegetables. When Matt was in chiropractic school, he sat under the training of Dr. Chestnut, who taught him to have fresh fiber, in the form of a vegetable or fruit, before consuming other food because it prepares the digestive system for what is to come.

When I learned this "fresh fiber first" principle, it challenged my view of vegetables. Instead of seeing them as something I had to eat to lose weight, I started to view them as something that would fuel my body for my day. This simple mindset shift was small but mighty, and in turn my habits changed for the better.

Where our minds go, our bodies and lives will follow. Romans 12:2 tells us, "Do not conform to the pattern of this world, but be transformed by the renewing of your mind. Then you will be able to test and approve what God's will is—his good, pleasing and perfect will."

Notice the word *renewing* in this verse. The meaning of the Greek word here is "washing of renewal through the Holy Spirit."[1] We cannot renew our minds in our own strength. The power of the Holy Spirit is our only answer to having a sound mind about our body image.

> Where our minds go, our bodies and lives will follow.

Strong Body

This final area of healthy habits that align with God's Word is probably not what you envision when reading the term *strong body*. I've been called a "beast" multiple times in the gym because I am considered strong for a woman. I didn't think that was a compliment in the past, but now I embrace it because I love lifting heavy weights. But that's not the kind of strength I'm referring to here.

Did you know your body can move in three planes of motion? The transverse plane divides the body into superior and inferior halves, allowing for rotational movement. The sagittal plane divides the body into left and right halves, enabling forward and backward movement. And the frontal plane divides the body into front and back halves, allowing for side-to-side movement.

I don't want to get too deep into human anatomy, but my point in mentioning these planes of motion is that most injuries result from overtraining in one plane and undertraining in another.

The human body is one of the most beautifully complex pieces of all God's creation. I love to study the parallels between God's creation and scientific discoveries. While this isn't a training program to teach you how to cross-train your body, it is vital to cross-train your spirit concerning the body. First Timothy 4:8 describes it best: "For physical training is of some value, but godliness has value for all things, holding promise for both the present life and the life to come."

Physical training has value. It can increase endorphins, decrease depression, prevent heart disease, and so much more. Still, without a strong spirit inside the body, we build an empire that will not last.

First Chronicles 29:15 says, "We are here for only a moment, visitors and strangers in the land as our ancestors were before us. Our days on earth are like a passing shadow, gone so soon without a trace" (NLT). No matter how hard we work out or diet or fight the aging process, the physical body is fading away. For that reason, I encourage you to choose movement that brings you joy. Move your body in ways that make you feel empowered and that draw you closer to Jesus. Then your workout is an act of worship!

Body Image Blueprint

Now it's time to pray, process, and praise through what we just learned.

Let's Pray

Father, thank You for the alarm systems You've put within my body to alert me when something is wrong. Please forgive me for ignoring my body when she tells me to slow down or change directions. Restore my health and union with You. I submit my heart, mind, and body to You. In Jesus' name, amen.

Use the space provided to write your own prayer.

Pause to Process

1. Consider keeping a "habits journal" for a week or two.

2. Which of your habits honor God?

_____

_____

_____

_____

_____

3. Which ones might you need to give up?

_____

_____

_____

_____

_____

Strong Foundation Verses

Use the following scriptural truths to strengthen your foundation. Consider saying them aloud, taking a picture of them to reference, or writing one that stands out on a sticky note and putting it somewhere you will see it daily.

- You have the right to do anything, but not everything is beneficial. (1 Cor. 10:23–24)
- "Whatever you do, do it all for the glory of God." (1 Cor. 10:31)
- "Physical training is of some value, but godliness has value for all things." (1 Tim. 4:8)
- "Whatever you do, work at it with all your heart, as working for the Lord, not for human[s]." (Col. 3:23)
- "Do not grieve the Holy Spirit of God." (Eph. 4:30)

Let's Rest in God's Word

As you complete this chapter's therapeutic coloring activity, meditate on the key verse and thank God for your body—exactly as it is today.

WHATEVER YOU DO, DO IT ALL FOR THE GLORY OF GOD.

SO WHETHER YOU EAT OR DRINK OR WHATEVER YOU DO,
DO IT ALL FOR THE GLORY OF GOD.
1 CORINTHIANS 10:31

Chapter 15

The Only One on the Block

As noted previously, our family is in the process of building our first home from the ground up, exactly like we want it. Custom builds are interesting because the builders tell us we can choose whatever design we want for our family. Yet, when I brought up a specific style I like, our architect suggested we go with something else that wouldn't stick out too much from the other homes. In other words, we can be unique, but not so much that we look out of place in our neighborhood.

Much like this home-building experience, we live in a world that tells us to be unique, yet there can be pressure to not be *too* different from the norm. I learned this lesson about my unique body in gym class in the third grade.

I have never been a fan of wearing jean shorts. All that stiff material clinging to my stomach and chafing my thighs? No thanks. Aside from jean shorts being my least-favorite item to wear, the truth is that I experienced some "small *t*" trauma around them.

It happened when I stayed the night with a friend and forgot to pack clothes to wear to school. My friend's body was built much differently than mine. She was tall and thin; I was short and curvy. The only thing we could find in her closet that I could get over my thighs were her jean shorts. There wasn't much wiggle room in these shorts, but they would have to work.

Like most third graders, I didn't think through everything in my day before going to school. My heart sank when my teacher announced it was time to go to gym class. How in the world could I run, jump, or skip in these tight shorts? To make matters worse, I found myself in the front row during our warm-up exercises. I crept slowly into the exercises, praying my shorts would stay in place. Just when I started to relax, I heard a giant *RIIIIIIP!* We were doing "grasshoppers," and as I bent over, those shorts, which were already glued to my body, ripped right up the back seam. I was left standing in the front row, displaying my cream underwear with hot pink hearts. Of course, my face was probably hotter pink than those hearts. The students behind me started to snicker, and I immediately ran to the perimeter, turned my back toward the wall, and slowly shuffled out of the gym.

My PE teacher sent me to the nurse to get a change of clothes. Unfortunately, the lost and found had nothing that would fit, so the school called my parents to bring a new outfit. This was before the time of cell phones, and my parents were unable to be reached on their landline. The nurse did the next best thing she knew at that moment. She wrapped me in a blanket while she "fixed" my shorts by safety pinning the entire seam. I wrestled my way back into those already-tight jean shorts, careful not to get poked by the pins. The row of twelve safety pins didn't wholly bring the seam back together, so I wore them the rest of the day with my hot pink hearts peeking through. That was the longest day of my third-grade life.

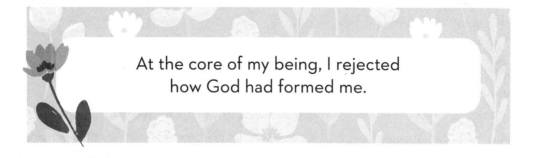

At the core of my being, I rejected
how God had formed me.

My third-grade self couldn't help but wonder why I was built differently from most of my peers. I remember looking down at my thighs and thinking, *If you weren't so big, this wouldn't have happened.*

That was just one of the "small *t*" traumas in my early years that sent me on a quest to change the shape of my body. While I couldn't control my height, I eventually learned how to manage my width. At the core of my being, I rejected how God had formed me. We're going to look at what the Bible says about His unique design for each of us. But first, I want to put on my cheerleader hat and share some words I would have said to my younger self, words I finally embrace almost three decades later.

Hey, strong girl. You are built strong to be a torch carrier of God's Word. While your body is beautiful, your purpose does not rise and fall on the appearance of your body. Your heavenly Father sees you and loves you just the way you are. Stand tall and confident, and show up fully as He made you. Our world is counting on you to be who God created you to be.

What would you say to your younger self about your unique design?

Therapist Thoughts

Individual characteristics can influence body image. For example, high self-esteem contributes to healthy body image, whereas perfectionist tendencies contribute to unhealthy body image. What unique characteristics has God deposited in you that positively influence your body image?

Temple Truths

This idea of unique design goes far beyond the appearance of our bodies. The more I get to know my strengths and weaknesses, the more I am blown away by how God is in every detail of our lives. Everything from the sound of our voices to our personality types was hand-selected by Him to serve a specific purpose.

As a young girl, I would often get in trouble in class for daydreaming. The teacher would say something that made my mind wander to a far-off place, and suddenly I'd be lost in thought while everyone else had moved on to the next task. Because I am a deep thinker, I can sometimes be mistaken for being cold or distant, when in reality I listen intently to what is being said and then look at it from all sides. This ability to see a different perspective has equipped me to be a good counselor and communicator.

The first blog post I ever wrote was called "Be Your Color," and it stemmed from a coloring activity I'd completed with my daughters. One afternoon, as I was sharing my insecurities with the Lord, He gave me an idea to ask my girls, whose ages at the time were four and six, to color pictures. In the first picture, I instructed my daughter to color it all one color. She chose the color brown. In the second picture, I told my other daughter to use as many colors as she wanted.

Their finished products were breathtakingly different. The picture that was one color lacked clarity and unique character; everything just blended in and lost its original form. The picture that was filled with multiple colors was vibrant, and each unique part jumped off the page.

This image is a breathtaking visual of how God created us all unique and assigned us each a particular color, or purpose, that only we can fulfill. When we compare our bodies, gifts, talents, careers, and passions to others and try to be their "color," we miss the call on our lives and fail to display God's true beauty to the world.

Did you know the number of color combinations in the world is endless? This is because color is affected by the amount of lighting, other colors in the surrounding, and even the person viewing the colors. Can you imagine how boring and dull our world would look if God had created only one color?

> When we compare our bodies, gifts, talents, careers, and passions to others and try to be their "color," we miss the call on our lives and fail to display God's true beauty to the world.

Let's apply this principle to body image.

Genesis 1:27 tells us we were created in the image of God: "So God created mankind in his own image, in the image of God he created them, male and female he created them."

This verse has been one I've meditated on often throughout my life. It causes confusion when we try to fit God into the cookie-cutter shape of an image defined by the current culture. Let's break down this word *image* as it relates to our body image.

The phrase *body image* is defined as "a subjective picture or mental image of one's own physical appearance."[1] The word *subjective* means "based on or influenced by personal feelings, tastes, or opinions."[2] The problem with this definition of body image is that it does not reflect the heart of God or His image at all. His image is *not* influenced by personal feelings, tastes, or opinions.

As I did some digging on this word *image* in the Bible, do you know what I found at the root? *Jesus.*

- "The Son is the image of the invisible God, the firstborn over all creation." (Col. 1:15)
- "The god of this age has blinded the minds of unbelievers, so that they cannot see the light of the gospel that displays the glory of Christ, who is the image of God." (2 Cor. 4:4)
- "And we all, who with unveiled faces contemplate the Lord's glory, are being transformed into his image with ever-increasing glory, which comes from the Lord, who is the Spirit." (2 Cor. 3:18)

Let's reflect on these verses concerning the illustration I shared about the "Be Your Color" activity. Just as natural light causes colors to be expressed differently, so does the light of Jesus.

We just read in 2 Corinthians 4:4 that the god of this age has blinded the minds of unbelievers but that the light of the gospel radiates the glory of Jesus. This, my dear friends, is excellent news for believers! It means that when I submit my heart and life to Jesus, His radiance shines through me, and I am then (and only then) a reflection of the image of God. Without Jesus, this quest for a healthy body image will fall short every time. If you want to be the true color that God created you to be, start by letting Jesus shine His light through you.

While there are things we may wish looked different on our bodies, God does not make mistakes. He is the Master Creator, and to reject my body is to reject His creation.

Recently, the Lord brought this truth to light as I worked on a project with my daughters. A talent I do not possess is artistic creativity. This includes knitting or sewing of any kind. But my oldest daughter is gifted in this area, and occasionally I will try to work alongside her. She recently taught me how to cross-stitch. We ordered beginner kits for kids that I couldn't mess up. *Or so we thought.* These were so easy; all I had to do was follow the pattern. The colors and lines were already laid out, and my only job was to stitch. I was moving, grooving, and feeling quite proud of myself. Until I got to the end of the color I'd been working on and asked my daughter to help me thread a new one. She looked down and exclaimed, "Mom! What did you do?!"

Apparently, I had stitched my needle into the pattern. The only way out was to cut the thread, which unraveled all my hard work. We had a good giggle that I had somehow found a way to mess up a beginner's art project.

That's when it hit me. Numbers 23:19 says, "God is not human, that he should lie, not a human being, that he should change his mind. Does he speak and then not act? Does he promise and not fulfill?" When God knit us together in our mother's womb, He did not have the perspective our world has regarding what we should look like. His thoughts and ways are so much higher than ours (see Isa. 55:8–9). If God speaks and says we are fearfully and wonderfully made (see Ps. 139:14), then it is finished. Case closed.

But know this: if it matters to you, it matters to God. God cares about the details. Bring your worries, doubts, and questions to Him. Let Him show you the purpose behind your unique design. You are not too much or too little. You are precisely as God knit you to be.

My unique design of thick thighs and a muscular build has forced me to face body image battles head-on. But … if I hadn't gone through those battles, I wouldn't be writing this book today. God knew this journey would prepare me to be a torch carrier, sharing the good news that Jesus paid for it all … even our body image battles.

Body Image Blueprint

Now it's time to pray, process, and praise through what we just learned.

Let's Pray

Father, thank You for knitting me together in my mother's womb. I admit I struggle to accept the unique design of my body. Show me how You see me. Jesus, fill me with Your light that I may bear the image of God. In Jesus' name, amen.

Use the space provided to write your own prayer.

Pause to Process

1. Earlier in this chapter, I shared a letter I would have loved to give to my third-grade self about her true beauty. Put on your cheerleading hat and do the same for yourself. Use the space provided to write it out.

_____

_____

_____

_____

_____

_____

---

2. Now read your letter aloud, and receive it over yourself today.

Strong Foundation Verses

Use the following scriptural truths to strengthen your foundation. Consider saying them aloud, taking a picture of them to reference, or writing one that stands out on a sticky note and putting it somewhere you will see it daily.

- All things were made through Christ. (John 1:3)
- He knit you together in your mother's womb. (Ps. 139:13)
- God is not a human that He should lie or change His mind. He keeps His promises. (Num. 23:19)
- Your unveiled face contemplates the Lord's glory. (2 Cor. 3:18)
- Your new self is being renewed in the image of your Creator. (Col. 3:10)

Let's Rest in God's Word

You will notice there are two images to color today. Color one with just one shade. Then, get creative with the other. Now you have your very own illustration of why your unique design in our world matters!

BE YOUR COLOR

Unit 5 Counselor's Cornerstone

Strengthening Your Foundation

In this unit, we will strengthen our foundation by reflecting on what it means to be made in God's image. Have you ever considered that the only way we reflect His image is by Jesus living within us? In our strength and human power, it's impossible to reflect the image and nature of God truly. But when Jesus entered the scene, He changed everything. He took the pressure off for us to perform or strive to be image-bearers of God. Jesus shining through us is a reflection of God's image.

Let's take a few verses from this unit's chapters and write them out. Then meditate on what they mean to you and your body image.

1. **Write Genesis 1:27.** Reflect on what attributes of God's image you see in yourself. Write them down and return to them when you need a reminder of your authentic image.

_____

_____

_____

_____

2. **Write Isaiah 64:8.** Reflect on the unique design God, the potter, gave you, from the top of your head down to your pinky toes. Think about whatever is true, noble, and worthy of praise for your design. Praise God for putting breath in your body and giving you life.

_____

_____

_____

3. **Write Colossians 3:10.** Often, we focus so much on our body image that we fail to see the image of our Creator. Write down everything you love about God. Spend time in His Word and learn about His character. Write down anything you find, and reflect on it when your faith needs strengthening.

_____

_____

_____

_____

_____

Counselor's Chat

In the unit 5 video, I'm speaking life over you in the area of seeing God reflected in your body image. I will walk you through this unit's counseling activity and end with a prayer of blessing over your body image. You can access the video with the QR code on page 22.

Therapy Toolbox

Mirror gratitude techniques are often used in group therapy for body image. This tool can help shift our focus from any negative physical attributes we see to the positive ones. But without a biblical view, we can easily slip back into our old way of seeing ourselves. Use the "In His Image" mirror template and the following prompts to create your own masterpiece:

- What do you see when you look in the mirror? Write all the things that come to mind on your mirror.
- Strike through any of the negative attributes, and ask God what He sees instead.
- Highlight or circle the positive attributes. Ask God to show you why He designed you that way. I sense He will give you a prophetic word that you can cling to.
- Do you see Jesus reflected in your image?

In His image

Unit 6

The Covering

Chapter 16

God's Love and Jesus' Blood

As Matt and I build our house, we have to make budget decisions. While I would love to skimp on the roof because all roofs look the same to me, I know we have to make a wise choice about what covers our home to protect it from damage imposed by storms and our scorching Texas heat.

I turned to Matt's grandfather, who advised, "Rachael, when choosing how much you want to spend on a roof, you need to decide how long you plan on staying in the home. If you plan on being here for ten-plus years, it would be wise to make the investment up front for a solid roof."

How long do you plan on staying in this body of yours? While I am eager to meet Jesus one day, I know for now I am called to stay here on earth to be a light in a lost world. This chapter isn't going to give you ten steps to keep your body in tip-top condition, though I do believe in stewarding our health. Instead, it's going to provide you with tools to see and treat your body the way God does.

God's kingdom is one full of grace, compassion, love, forgiveness, and mercy. I have spent much of my life treating my body in every way opposite of those words. Let's flip the script on how we've learned to see our struggles in this area of body image.

Do you remember the structural story I told in chapter 4 about the cute guy who shamed me in the cafeteria? What I didn't share the first time was why my family had moved to Florida in the first place.

My dad was a pastor, and through a series of events, my parents felt the Lord calling our family to be part of the Brownsville Revival. My entire world was shaken when we moved from our small town in Oklahoma, where I knew everyone, to the "big city" of Pensacola, where I knew no one. This revival was unlike anything I had ever experienced. Services were held seven days a week, and people were so hungry for God, they were willing to stand in line for hours to ensure they got a seat when the doors opened!

Because my dad served as one of their traveling evangelists, I never did have to wait in that line, but I was in the building from the time the service started, around 7:00 p.m., until after midnight. Every night, I would watch as people leaped over pews to run to the altar and give their lives to Jesus. It was in that revival that I gave my heart to the Lord and was baptized. I experienced such a radical transformation that even the kids at school noticed I was different. I was "on fire for Jesus," and I wanted everyone to know about Him.

That is, *until* my body image struggles started to creep in.

The boy in the lunchroom was the beginning of my struggles, and the attacks kept coming—even after I returned to my school in Oklahoma. I see now the Enemy used my insecurities to lead me away from my relationship with God and His calling on my life. In time, I became more obsessed with my appearance and less focused on Jesus. Instead of following Him, I wandered down lonely paths, chasing the body I thought would earn me the right to be loved. I couldn't see that all the while, Jesus was right there, waiting for me to return to His unconditional love.

Therapist Thoughts

God's love. You can't buy it. You can't lose it. It is unconditional, with no strings attached. It is not dependent on your looks or any measure of performance. Love can't be earned. It's freely given. You can find it anywhere. It's for everyone. Including you, no matter who you are, where you're from, or what you've done. His love covers it all. (Dr. Linda Hoover)

What I didn't learn in that revival is that God's love never stops chasing us down. Somewhere along the way, I believed the lie that if I was no longer walking in freedom, then

I'd obviously messed up too much to come back to the Lord in whatever area I was struggling with. While we cannot lose God's love or our salvation, we can walk away from freedom.

If we want our body image house to be covered with a roof that will hold up under pressure, we must clothe ourselves in God's love and Jesus' blood. Let's dive into what that looks like practically in this chapter's Temple Truths.

Temple Truths

One of the reasons I wrestled with being a voice in this body image area was that I am still walking out my freedom daily. While the struggle continues, the Lord has given me a powerful tool: I have learned to rest in and receive His unconditional love.

Psalm 103:8 says, "The LORD is compassionate and gracious, slow to anger, abounding in love."

That phrase "abounding in love" can be expressed in a single Hebrew word, *chesed*, meaning "goodness, kindness." This is only the tip of the iceberg in exploring the Bible and what we find about God's love for us.

If we look at the character of God throughout all of Scripture, we see this theme of His goodness and kindness toward humanity. It brings me to tears to think that the Lord would be good to me even when I turn away from Him. It's a love that most of us don't know from humans, yet God shows that love to us every day, no matter our failures or sins.

He loves you, my friend. As you think about the covering of your body, cover yourself in His love. It looks like kindness, grace, and mercy, even when you don't get it right. He will never stop chasing you down with His love. Add this simple praise and promise from Psalm 36:7 to your daily routine: "How priceless is your unfailing love, O God! People take refuge in the shadow of your wings."

The second covering that must be on our body image roof is Jesus' blood. We know that Jesus died for our sins, but I think many Christians are walking in bondage because we fail to activate the gift of the Holy Spirit. Remember, when Jesus died, He sent the Spirit to be our helper and friend.

Check out these words directly from Jesus: "Do not let your hearts be troubled. You believe in God; believe also in me. My Father's house has many rooms; if that were not so, would I have told you that I am going there to prepare a place for you?" (John 14:1–2).

He goes on to say, "And I will ask the Father, and he will give you another advocate to help you and be with you forever—the Spirit of truth. The world cannot accept him, because it neither sees him nor knows him. But you know him, for he lives with you and will be in you" (vv. 16–17).

These words from Jesus tell us two things. First, His Father's house has many rooms. This means there is space for everyone, no matter our age, shape, size, ethnicity, or number on the scale. The only requirement on our part to enter is to accept Jesus as our Lord and Savior. Next, He sent the Holy Spirit to be our advocate, or helper, who will never leave us. This promise is mind-boggling; we have a helper with us always. We never have to do this life alone! And when we feel defeated or overwhelmed, all we have to do is ask the Holy Spirit to help in our time of need.

You know those times when you have a feeling in your gut that you aren't supposed to do something? That's usually the Holy Spirit waving red flags to stop you before you end up in a bad situation. When we ignore the red flags, we reject the Holy Spirit, and we usually suffer the consequences.

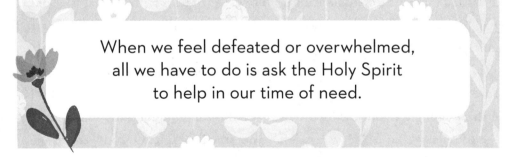

When we feel defeated or overwhelmed, all we have to do is ask the Holy Spirit to help in our time of need.

Just a few days ago, I felt the Holy Spirit tell me not to attend a particular event. I ignored my gut and went anyway, expecting to have fun. Needless to say, I ended up in an uncomfortable situation, and I was exhausted the next day, losing my typical Sabbath day of rest. While my consequences were short-lived, there have been other times in my life when I ignored the Holy Spirit's direction and found myself in more severe consequences. Like a built-in bodyguard, the Spirit warns and redirects for our protection. Whether I listen is my choice, but either way, He is always there, ready to help me get back on track when I mess up.

What does this have to do with body image? I believe the power of the Trinity is the only covering that will keep us on track when it comes to our bodies. Remember in chapter 7 when we discussed the Triangle Effect of our thoughts, feelings, and behaviors? Let's use that same analogy for the Father, Son, and Holy Spirit. I call this the Trinity Effect:

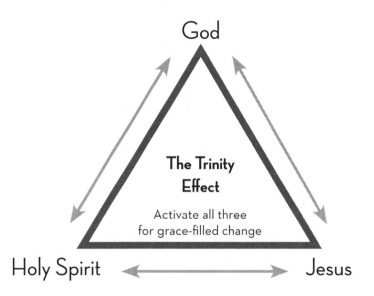

We must activate the Father, Son, and Holy Spirit if we want to maintain true freedom in this area of body image. The Father covers us with His love, Jesus covers us with His blood, and the Holy Spirit gives us gut-level guidance to help us walk in freedom daily. To remove one of these key pieces would be to limp our way to freedom, which is not what God promises us.

Activating the Holy Spirit in the area of our body image looks like inviting Him into every decision we make—from what we eat, to how we spend our time and resources, and even who we follow on social media.

What looks like freedom for me may not look like freedom for you. I've heard well-meaning Christian leaders warn against specific exercise or eating programs. It's not my job to be the body image police or to try to be the voice of the Holy Spirit to you. I would rather teach you how to hear His voice for yourself, so you can consult with Him on every decision you make.

The answer is already within you. Trust your gut.

If something feels off about a particular program, don't do it. If, like me, you ignored the voice of the Holy Spirit when He tried to warn you not to do it, stop, ask forgiveness, and redirect. The Holy Spirit convicts us to redirect us, and this is the essence of grace. The Enemy of our souls condemns and brings confusion. The covering of God's love, Jesus' blood, and our helper, the Holy Spirit, is one we can't afford to live without. Will you receive them today?

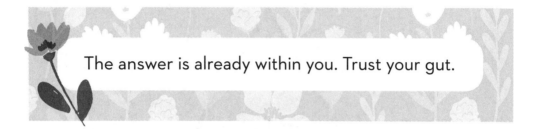

The answer is already within you. Trust your gut.

Body Image Blueprint

Now it's time to pray, process, and praise through what we just learned.

Let's Pray

Father, Jesus, Holy Spirit, thank You for covering my body image and life. I submit to Your authority. God, thank You for sending Jesus to die on the cross for my sins. Jesus, thank You for Your blood that has set me free. Holy Spirit, I receive You as my helper. Help me to walk in freedom in this area of body image. Give me wisdom in how to steward my body in a way that is pleasing to You. I choose to follow You. In Jesus' name, amen.

Use the space provided to write your own prayer.

Pause to Process

Do you struggle to trust your gut? If so, you aren't alone. One of the most common questions I hear is, "How do I learn to trust my gut?" First, we have to listen. Second, we have to practice.

Just as with building any muscles in our bodies, it takes time. Use the following questions to journal and work your "trust your gut" muscles.

1. Write about a time you had a gut feeling about something or someone and you didn't listen. What were the consequences of not listening to your gut?

_____

_____

_____

_____

_____

_____

_____

_____

_____

_____

_____

_____

_____

_____

2. Write about a time you did listen to your gut. What did it protect you from?

_____

_____

_____

_____

_____

_____

_____

_____

_____

_____

_____

_____

3. Do you think your gut is trustworthy? Why or why not? Trust is built over time. Try listening to your gut on small decisions, and the trust will increase. Ask the Holy Spirit to give you wisdom and discernment.

_____

_____

_____

_____

_____

_____

Strong Foundation Verses

Use the following scriptural truths to strengthen your foundation. Consider saying them aloud, taking a picture of them to reference, or writing one that stands out on a sticky note and putting it somewhere you will see it daily.

- His unfailing love is priceless. (Ps. 36:7)
- "The LORD is compassionate and gracious, slow to anger, abounding in love." (Ps. 103:8)
- "These three remain: faith, hope and love. But the greatest of these is love." (1 Cor. 13:13)
- The Lord takes great delight in you. In His love, He does not rebuke you. (Zeph. 3:17)
- God showed His love by sending His Son that we might live through Him. (1 John 4:9–10)
- The Father lavishes you with His love. (1 John 3:1)
- Hope does not put you to shame because God's love has been poured into your heart. (Rom. 5:5)

Let's Rest in God's Word

As you complete this chapter's therapeutic coloring activity, meditate on the key verse and thank God for your body—exactly as it is today.

THESE THINGS GOD HAS REVEALED TO US
THROUGH THE SPIRIT.
1 CORINTHIANS 2:10 (ESV)

Chapter 17

God's Grace and Jesus' Face

When I found out I was pregnant with our first child, I ate for two as though my baby had an adult appetite. All the years of withholding from foods were now over as I finally had an excuse to eat everything I wanted. My poor diet caused me to get preeclampsia toward the end of my pregnancy, and due to my high blood pressure, we were forced to induce labor a few days before my due date.

I had read all the books and talked to all the women about what to expect in childbirth. Some moms shared stories of being in and out of labor and delivery within a few hours, while others told tales that made me want to opt out of giving birth. With all of my well-informed choices detailed in my birth plan, I was determined to be one of the in-and-out childbirth stories, with zero complications.

Then we arrived at the hospital, and the nurses began the induction.

Everything was going well at first, but before I knew what was happening, I was whisked away to the operating room for an emergency cesarean section. I remember lying on the operating table, fully awake, with a sheet blocking my view of the surgery taking place. I stared at the white, cold ceiling as I felt my body jerk around, thinking, *It wasn't supposed to go like this.*

The cry of our firstborn baby brought me back to reality, and a breath of relief washed over me when I met our beautiful, healthy baby girl. Matt was the first to hold her while the surgeons and nurses put me back together. The whole thing felt like an out-of-body experience with so many people working in and around my torso.

The days to follow in recovery brought a strange mixture of emotions. On the one hand, I was mesmerized by our perfect new baby. On the other hand, I felt shame around my body. Once again, I couldn't help but wonder what was wrong with me. Why hadn't my body performed like all the other women who'd shared their birthing stories with me? Not one of those women had told me about the possibility of a C-section.

> My hustling to take better care of myself wasn't what brought the breakthrough. The breakthrough came when I released control to God.

I felt betrayed by my body and thought if I had taken better care of myself, I wouldn't have had any difficulties giving birth. *I now know this isn't the truth,* but at the time, I struggled alone.

Just months after I delivered my daughter, Matt started school to become a chiropractor. During his studies, we were introduced to a new form of health care that was more preventative and utilized holistic alternatives in conjunction with traditional medicine. We began to focus on whole food nutrition (remember that "fresh fiber first" principle I mentioned in chapter 14?), dietary supplements, and chiropractic care. For the first time in my life, I saw food as my friend rather than an enemy I had to wrestle.

When I discovered I was expecting again, I knew things would be different this time. We found a doctor who would let me attempt a vaginal birth after a cesarean (VBAC). I ate all the right foods, exercised, and rested as needed. I was even given a book on childbirth that I read daily to set my mind right on delivering this baby naturally and vaginally. Our baby's due date came and went. Ten days after her due date, I finally went into labor. At the first sign of contractions, we rushed to the hospital because I was sure this delivery would be quick and easy. When we arrived, the nurse let me know I was barely dilated, and she discouraged me from attempting a VBAC for fear that it was too dangerous. My doctor told us to leave and return when contractions grew more intense.

Later that day, contractions had become consistent enough to justify a return to the hospital, and the doctor kept me that time. I continued to labor long and hard for several more hours. At about 9:00 p.m., my doctor told us that if I didn't start to progress soon, we would need to do a C-section. My heart sank. I felt like I was about to have the rug pulled out from under me again. I had done everything right with this pregnancy, so why wouldn't my body perform?!

After we received this news, my husband and mom prayed over the baby and me. As we prayed, I whispered a simple prayer, "Lord, I release control to You. I am at peace with whatever needs to happen at this moment. Please just keep our baby safe."

Within minutes of that prayer, I told the nurse I felt like I needed to go to the bathroom.

I know now that means the baby is on the way. My nurse told me to wait until she got my doctor. I tried to wait, but two pushes and my daughter came flying out. My doctor was rounding the corner, putting his gloves on, and arrived just in time to deliver her. While it's true I got my desired result and delivered my daughter vaginally, it was never really about how my daughter was born. It was about learning to let go of control and surrender it to the Lord. My hustling to take better care of myself wasn't what brought the breakthrough. The breakthrough came when I released control to God.

Please don't get lost in the details of my story. I grieve as I type these words because so many precious women have experienced child loss, infertility, disappointments, miscarriage, sickness, trauma, and rejection in their bodies. I had a miscarriage about a year after the delivery of this baby, and that loss tested my faith in God unlike anything I had walked through before. If that's you, I am so sorry for your pain and loss. I am praying that God meets with you in this space as we gently look at what we have believed to be true about our bodies and God's amazing grace.

Therapist Thoughts

Take a moment to sit in the stillness of God's presence. Imagine grace being freely poured over you like a warm, fragrant oil. Breathe in deeply as it is absorbed into every thirsty cell. Notice any places where the oil does not soak in. Offer those areas to the Lord and allow His gentle grace to soften your soul until it is fully saturated and satisfied. (Dr. Linda Hoover)

Temple Truths

We discussed the importance of a solid roof in the previous chapter. Another covering essential to our sound body image house is God's grace. Before I knew how my second daughter's birth story would end, we had felt the Lord tell us her middle name was to be Grace. I didn't realize it foreshadowed what was to come in God showing *me* grace. Even though I'd messed up in my attempts to control the situation, He extended grace because that's who God is. He consistently gives us what we don't deserve.

The purpose of this chapter is to look at body image as something more profound than what we can see with our eyes. When things don't go as planned in our bodies, it is an attack on who we believe God to be, since we've established from Genesis 1:27 that we are made in His image. The darkest moments I've walked through in my body taught me a few simple truths about God's grace and Jesus' face.

First, God's grace is always available, and it is undeserved. The following definition of *grace* paints a beautiful picture:

> Nearly two-thirds (100 of 154) of the New Testament occurrences of *charis*, normally translated as "grace," are found in the Pauline letters. In Pauline usage, the word *charis* carries the basic sense of "favor" (cf. Heb *ḥēn*, "favor," and *ḥesed*, "loving kindness,") in the OT; and when God or Christ is its subject, acting in grace toward humankind, it is undeserved favor.[1]

The last line struck me: *it is undeserved favor.* The word *favor* as a verb means to "feel or show approval or preference for."[2] God's grace is literally Him showing approval and preference for us, even when we did nothing to deserve it. We cannot earn His grace. He distributes it freely.

Here's why this concept of grace is relevant to body image: we *will* mess up. Even those of us who teach body image principles will sometimes get it wrong. I still have days when I allow fear, lies, insecurity, doubt, and hustling to creep into my heart. I get to choose in those moments whether I will keep striving or turn back to God and let His grace wash over me.

The second thing I've learned is that Jesus' face releases God's grace. Second Corinthians 12:9 says, "But he said to me, 'My grace is sufficient for you, for my power is made perfect in weakness.' Therefore I will boast all the more gladly about my weaknesses so that Christ's power may rest on me."

I've heard this verse quoted often, and with good reason, because it brings peace. I first understood this when I helped Matt move an old dresser down our stairs.

We have a spiral staircase in our home, and if you've seen the *Friends* episode with Ross, Chandler, and Rachel trying to move a couch upstairs, you probably just chuckled. For those who don't know the scene, in an attempt to move a couch upstairs, Ross keeps yelling "PIVOT" while the three struggle to move the piece of furniture. Of course, they ultimately get stuck.

This was the scene playing out for us that day, except with a dresser. This particular dresser was an antique piece of furniture, and it was *heavy*. When we rounded the corner, I lost my grip and became pinned under the dresser. I couldn't say anything, but I locked eyes with Matt, and he immediately knew I was in trouble. His adrenaline kicked in, and he lifted the entire dresser off me, over his head, and carried it down the stairs.

When we lock eyes with Jesus, He picks up whatever is weighing us down and carries it; only, His adrenaline doesn't have to kick in, because He is not a mere man, whose power has limits.

> God's grace is literally Him showing approval and preference for us, even when we did nothing to deserve it. We cannot earn His grace. He distributes it freely.

The third thing I've learned from physical struggles is that God is our *defender*. Romans 16:20 says, "The God of peace will soon crush Satan under your feet. The grace of our Lord Jesus be with you."

There's that word *grace* again. But this time, it follows our God of peace crushing Satan. God defends against words spoken over our bodies that are not in line with His Word, as well as other things not from Him, like sickness and disease.

Let's start with how God defends the words spoken over us. God says your body is good. Remember in Genesis when God declared multiple times that everything He had made was good? That included Adam and Eve. We have an Enemy who tries to convince us otherwise. Our bodies being good is not contingent on how they look or perform. They are good because God says they are good. However, because God gives us free will, He can only defend what we allow Him to.

Have you ever considered letting God speak into your life about your body? He wants to protect it in ways only He can.

Next, God defends our health. Sickness and pain exist because we live in a fallen world. When we take responsibility for the failures in our bodies, we will also take the praise when they are performing well. We weren't meant to carry shame or praise. In sickness and in health, God is in control of our bodies, and He is the only one who deserves any honor or praise. Yes, it is a partnership, but our part is simply obedience.

First John 3:8 says, "The one who does what is sinful is of the devil, because the devil has been sinning from the beginning. The reason the Son of God appeared was to destroy the devil's work." Jesus appeared to destroy the Devil's work. Our obedience partnered with the power of Jesus is the combination needed to walk in victory and receive God's grace over our bodies.

What piece of this covering do you need to put on your body image house today?

Body Image Blueprint

Now it's time to pray, process, and praise through what we just learned.

Let's Pray

Father, thank You for the grace that You pour out, even when I don't deserve it. Jesus, I look to Your face as I receive God's grace. I release control of my body to You. Defend me from the Enemy's plans against me. Surround me with Your unconditional favor. In Jesus' name, amen.

Use the space provided to write your own prayer.

Pause to Process

Take time to process your raw, unedited thoughts and emotions on this topic of grace. Remember, the antidote to shame is grace.

1. In what situations do you have a hard time receiving God's grace?

_____

_____

_____

_____

_____

2. When is it hardest for you to extend grace to yourself and others?

_____
_____
_____
_____
_____
_____
_____

3. In the chart below, write any area where you feel shame, and combat that with truth about God's grace.

Shame	Grace
"I shouldn't have eaten that cupcake."	"I am no longer a slave to fear; I am a child of God."

Strong Foundation Verses

Use the following scriptural truths to strengthen your foundation. Consider saying them aloud, taking a picture of them to reference, or writing one that stands out on a sticky note and putting it somewhere you will see it daily.

- "He has saved us … because of his own purpose and grace." (2 Tim. 1:9)
- Out of His fullness we receive grace. (John 1:16)
- "The grace of God … offers salvation to all people." (Titus 2:11)
- His grace is sufficient, for His power is made perfect in weakness. (2 Cor. 12:9)
- It is by grace we are saved, not by works, so no one can boast. (Eph. 2:8–9)
- "Grace and peace [are] yours in abundance." (2 Pet. 1:2)
- We can approach God's throne of grace with confidence. (Heb. 4:16)
- "God opposes the proud but gives grace to the humble." (James 4:6 ESV)

Let's Rest in God's Word

As you complete this chapter's therapeutic coloring activity, meditate on the key verse and thank God for your body—exactly as it is today.

THE GOD OF PEACE WILL SOON CRUSH SATAN UNDER YOUR FEET.

THE GRACE OF OUR LORD JESUS BE WITH YOU.

ROMANS 16:20

Chapter 18

Find Your Body Image Neighborhood

Finding a community where I fit in has been a struggle for most of my life. While growing up, I tried to fit in with the athletes. But as you know by now, no matter how hard I tried, I couldn't keep up. My coaches and teammates would get frustrated when I kept everyone waiting. I eventually quit sports … in part due to an injury but also because I didn't feel welcome. In college, I would exercise alone at crazy hours of the night. This felt safe because no one could speak into the insanity of what I was doing to my body, but it left me feeling isolated. When I taught group fitness, I was known as one of the most demanding instructors at the facility, but I didn't look like any of the fit ones. I always had a bit of my mama pouch left from having babies. Again, I didn't fit the mold.

My first encounter with a body image community that made me feel welcome was Revelation Wellness. Yet even there I found myself wondering if I fit in. It wasn't because of anything the staff did or said; instead, it was my own insecurities finally getting confronted now that I was in a healthy community.

In that community, I learned that exercise is a "get to," not a "have to," and that I can listen to what my body needs. This went against everything I knew to be true. I had only learned that we spend hours working out to burn calories in hopes of shedding a few pounds. I had never stopped to ask my body what she needed or wanted.

This new truth created a battle within me. On the one hand, I love the feeling I get when I complete a hard workout. It is empowering to see my body lift heavier weights or run farther distances than I thought she could. On the other hand, I feel a need to pull back and be gentle to my body.

At one Revelation Wellness event, I confided in my dear friend Heather, admitting that I was having a hard time deciding what to do for the workout I was co-teaching. I confessed that sometimes I felt like I needed to shrink back in order to fit in. Heather set me straight and said words I will never forget: "Rachael, you do YOU." My wise friend saw the battle happening within me, and through her encouragement I learned that I can do it all … lift heavy, run hard, *and* pull back to be kind to my body. It's all a matter of having this area submitted to the Lord.

A healthy community will challenge you in the areas where you aren't lined up with the Lord. It will also empower you to show up fully as yourself. Here is a simple checklist to reference when looking for a healthy body image and fitness community.

Healthy Community	Unhealthy Community
Their core beliefs about body image line up with yours and, most importantly, the Lord's.	They pressure you with high expectations to follow their extreme program.
You recognize "fruit" in their lives.	They fail to extend grace to themselves and others.
They express humility and a willingness to admit when they make mistakes.	They use shame and fear to motivate.
They always point you back to Jesus.	They gossip or slander one another.
They offer unconditional love and acceptance.	They encourage behaviors that are rooted in disordered eating or other unhealthy habits.
You feel a sense of peace when you are around them.	They use power or influence to manipulate people.
They love their bodies where they are and teach you how to listen to yours.	The subtle message they teach leads you to believe your worth is in your body.

Fruit of the Spirit
love, joy, peace, patience,
kindness, goodness, faithfulness,
gentleness, self-control
(Galatians 5:22–23 ESV)

We could keep this "fruit of the Spirit" list going for quite a while. Did you notice how "perfection" isn't listed in the fruit? No person or community is perfect. But their submission to the Lord is critical.

The bottom line: Ask the Holy Spirit to show you which community He wants you to join. In some seasons, He has called me to communities full of other believers. In other seasons, He has planted me among unbelievers who don't have the same foundation, but I could stand alongside them because of my solid foundation.

He knows what you can or can't handle in every season. Trust Him to lead you to the right community.

Therapist Thoughts

We are made in the image of God; therefore, we have His relational DNA. We're wired for connection. When something or someone damages our "wiring," it doesn't have to be fatal or final. Taking the risk to restore relational cords can move us from isolation to consolation. (Dr. Linda Hoover)

Temple Truths

As an introvert, I don't naturally welcome this idea of being an active part of a community. It's not that I don't like people; I just really love being alone, because I can think more clearly and hear God's voice. However, God has been reminding me that community is not only a good idea, but it's His idea.

After God created Adam, He immediately declared that it wasn't good for Adam to be alone, so He created Eve to be his helper. From there, we see entire nations built and destroyed, and the common factor among them was the spiritual foundation of their leaders and their communities.

> A healthy community will challenge you in the areas where you aren't lined up with the Lord. It will also empower you to show up fully as yourself.

R. W. Wall describes the "biblical idea of community" as always situated on a theological axis balanced by two convictions: first, that a good God finds forsaken persons who are alienated from all that makes for hope and well-being and calls them into a covenant people reconciled to all that makes for peace and freedom; and, second, that this redeemed people then responds to God by embodying their experience of God's salvation in their relations with each other.[1]

We are the "redeemed people" who are called to embody our experience of God's salvation in our relations with one another. As we do this, we carry out Proverbs 27:17: "As iron sharpens iron, so one person sharpens another." But we must be in community with others for this sharpening to occur.

My family and I enjoy watching the TV show *Forged in Fire*. In each episode, bladesmiths are given different challenges to complete in a limited amount of time. The tensions are high as they rush to create something in an hour that normally would take them days to build in their own shops. Once, as I watched them run around, frantically sharpening their iron and hurrying processes that should take a long time, the Lord brought to memory this verse on iron sharpening iron.

I'm no expert bladesmith, but here are a few things I've noticed in watching that show that apply to this area of sharpening each other in our body image community:

- Sharpening is necessary. Regardless of a blade's beauty, it needs to hold up under the pressure of the stress tests. If we want to stand firm in our faith and not crumble under the pressures of this world, we must let ourselves be sharpened by other believers.
- Sharpening is hard. To achieve the best result in our lives, we must get comfortable with being uncomfortable.
- Sharpening takes skill. It will take time and experience to learn how to give and receive sharpening within our community. The act should be done in love, not fear or manipulation.

It's clear to see that being sharpened by others is an essential part of our Christian walk in any area of our lives. But what about being in a community with nonbelievers?

I just shared how I've had seasons where God planted me among nonbelievers. Sometimes we are planted in a job, school, or other community where we are the only believers. I used to think I needed to scream and run. Well, maybe not the screaming part, but I definitely ran. When I was a young girl in church, I remember the pastor quoting 2 Corinthians 6:14, which says, "Do not be yoked together with unbelievers." When I heard that verse, I thought he was saying "yolked"—like, with the yellow part of an egg. I would envision two people getting an egg cracked on their heads, with the yolk running down their faces and into their eyes. It made me giggle, and it left me confused as to why God would warn us of this, other than to protect our eyes from the yolk.

All joking aside, this verse comes from a passage warning against idolatry, which, if you remember from chapter 10, is a topic God takes quite seriously. The Merriam-Webster dictionary defines *yoke* as "a wooden bar or frame by which two draft animals (such as oxen) are joined at the heads or necks for working together."[2]

Notice the final words of that definition: "for working together."

There is a distinct difference between being in a community where we might be planted to shine God's light in a lost world and joining together or being yoked for a common goal. My husband and I are yoked together in marriage. My kids are yoked to us as we lead our family. I am yoked together with other believers who are torch lighters in this biblical body image movement. I am yoked with Christ. This is my favorite yoke because Jesus says in Matthew 11:30, "For my yoke is easy and my burden is light."

I've also been unequally yoked with friends, past romantic interests, and leaders in the fitness industry. Since the beginning of time, the Lord has been bailing humankind out of unequal yokings.

Let's look at what He told the children of Israel as He led them to freedom in Exodus 6:6–7: "Therefore, say to the Israelites: 'I am the LORD, and I will bring you *out from under the yoke* of the Egyptians. I will free you from being slaves to them, and I will redeem you with an outstretched arm and with mighty acts of judgment. I will take you as my own people, and I will be your God. Then you will know that I am the LORD your God, who brought you *out from under the yoke* of the Egyptians."

See there? Twice He used the phrase "out from under the yoke."

If God brought the Israelites out from under the yoke of the Egyptians, He can bring us out from whatever yoke we are under. These yokes aren't always with other people. Sometimes we can be yoked with oppression, depression, anxiety, fear, and any other spirit that is not from God. This is where the iron sharpening iron comes in.

The greatest iron sharpener is God's Word. Hebrews 4:12 says, "For the word of God is alive and active. Sharper than any double-edged sword, it penetrates even to dividing soul and spirit, joints and marrow; it judges the thoughts and attitudes of the heart."

If you don't yet have a healthy community, get into God's Word. It will sharpen and reveal anything in your heart that needs to be addressed.

My prayer for this chapter is that you will see the importance of finding a healthy body image community. The right community can offer crucial covering for your body image house, especially when storms come your way. When you are down, discouraged, or tempted to walk away from the truth, your body image community can sharpen you with God's love and grace, empowering you to keep fighting the good fight.

Future generations are depending on you. Will you stand with this community of biblical body image warriors? We've saved a seat just for *you*.

> To join the Image RESTored community, scan the QR code on page 255.

Body Image Blueprint

Now it's time to pray, process, and praise through what we just learned.

Let's Pray

Father, thank You that community was Your idea. Draw me to a community of believers who will sharpen me, and give me the skills to sharpen them. Give me wisdom concerning whom I yoke myself to. Empower me to be a torch carrier in my generation. Give me the strength to show up when I want to hide. In Jesus' name, amen.

Use the space provided to write your own prayer.

Pause to Process

1. What community is God drawing you to in this season?

_____

_____

_____

_____

_____

_____

_____

_____

_____

_____

2. In what ways do you hope that community will encourage you to stay the course when you begin to wander?

_____

_____

_____

_____

_____

_____

_____

_____

_____

_____

3. What else would you add to the list of important things for you in a community?

_____

_____

_____

_____

_____

_____

_____

_____

_____

_____

Strong Foundation Verses

Use the following scriptural truths to strengthen your foundation. Consider saying them aloud, taking a picture of them to reference, or writing one that stands out on a sticky note and putting it where you will see it daily.

- "Confess your sins to each other and pray for each other." (James 5:16)
- "A friend loves at all times, and a brother is born for a time of adversity." (Prov. 17:17)
- "As iron sharpens iron, so one person sharpens another." (Prov. 27:17)
- Where two or three gather in His name, He is there with them. (Matt. 18:20)
- Do not give up meeting together, but encourage one another. (Heb. 10:25)
- "Two are better than one, because they have a good return for their labor.… A cord of three strands is not quickly broken." (Eccl. 4:9, 12b)

Let's Rest in God's Word

As you complete this chapter's therapeutic coloring activity, meditate on the key verse and thank God for your body—exactly as it is today.

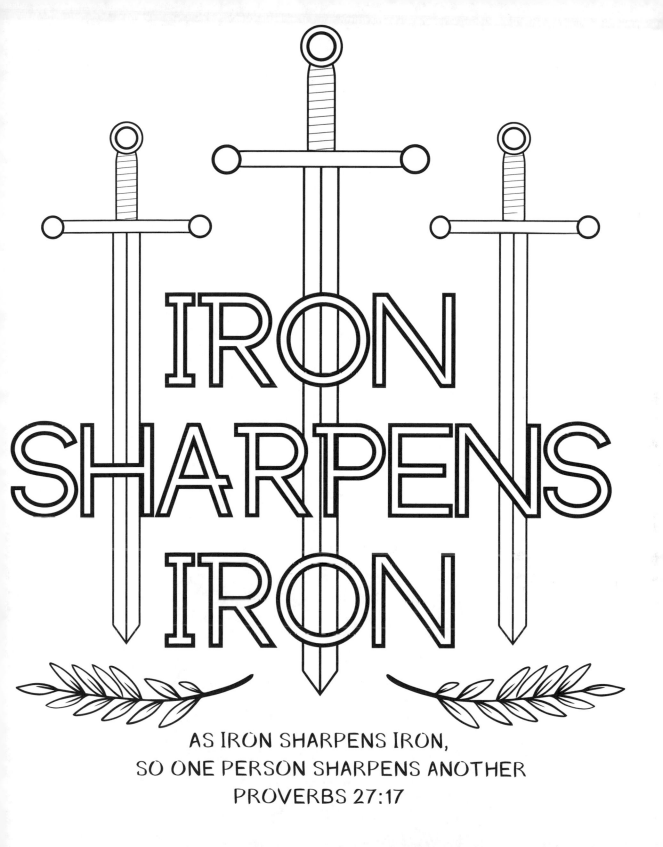

AS IRON SHARPENS IRON,
SO ONE PERSON SHARPENS ANOTHER
PROVERBS 27:17

Unit 6 Counselor's Cornerstone

Strengthening Your Foundation

There is a reason 1 Corinthians 13:13 says, "And now these three remain: faith, hope and love. But the greatest of these is love." God brings up this topic of love over and over in His Word because it sums up His heart for His people. He loves you so much, my friend. He not only gave up His only Son to die for you, but He keeps chasing you down with His unconditional love. The more we know and receive the love of God, the less we feel the need to earn love.

Let's write the following three verses and receive God's love.

1. Write Psalm 36:7. Cling to this verse when you feel vulnerable, afraid, or lonely in the area of body image.

_____

_____

_____

_____

_____

2. Write Psalm 109:26. This is a great verse to pray when you are struggling with your body image. Cling to God's unfailing love.

_____

_____

_____

_____

3. Write Zephaniah 3:17. Have you ever had anyone rejoice over *you* with singing? What a gift that the King of kings rejoices over us! Receive that love today.

_____

_____

_____

_____

_____

Counselor's Chat

In the unit 6 video, I'm walking you through how to build a healthy community using My Community Wheel. I will speak life over you about God's love and invite you into a special opportunity. You can access the video with the QR code on page 22.

Therapy Toolbox

As a counselor, one of my jobs is to ensure that my clients have a robust support system. One of my college professors, Dr. Linda Hoover, gave me the best illustration of how to build community, using a wagon wheel.

Have you ever seen the wheel on a wagon (perhaps in an old photo or movie)? Each wheel has several spokes that hold the wheel in place. If a wheel had only one spoke, it would fall apart under pressure.

Let's apply this to your community. Each spoke represents a relationship in your life; the more spokes on your community wheel, the stronger the support. When one spoke falls off, it's not a huge deal if you have other support. But if not enough spokes frame the wheel, the entire wheel might collapse under pressure.

In the last chapter of this book, we discussed the importance of surrounding yourself with supportive people in your body image community. Use these prompts to fill in your wheel:

- Write any healthy body image community you already have on the wheel's spokes. Examples include friends, family, church, a healthy workout group, or an online community.

- Next, examine your wheel. Does it seem strong? Are almost all the spokes filled in?
- Are any of the spokes filled in with people or communities that aren't supportive?
- Ask God to show you areas you could invest in to make your community wheel more stable.
- Can you be a spoke on someone else's body image wheel of community?

MY COMMUNITY WHEEL

Afterword

The Final Walk-Through

You did it! I am so proud of you for rebuilding your body image from the ground up.

When a home is complete, the new homeowners take a final walk-through to make sure everything is in order before the contractor signs over the house. This body image restoration has been a journey and will continue to be for the rest of our lives. But the good news is you now have tools to be victorious!

As I mentioned in the introduction, keep this book within arm's reach and go back to any chapters you might need to process further.

Reflect on these three questions as you take your final walk-through:

1. *How is my heart?* This is a powerful question I often ask my kids. If your heart doesn't feel right about an area, ask the Lord to place a pin on what is off.
2. *How are my words?* Luke 6:45 reminds us that "the mouth speaks what the heart is full of." When you aren't sure about the answer to the previous question about your heart, listen to the words you speak about your body. My husband once said, "Stop talking about my wife that way" when I spoke idle words over my body. Our words are an indicator of what's happening in our hearts.
3. *What foundation am I standing on?* The theme throughout this book has consistently brought us back to the foundation of God's Word.

When God points out something not in alignment in our hearts, the best way to restore it is to get in His Word. Let His truth, love, and grace wash over your body.

With these questions in mind, let's go back to the same image introduced in unit 1, only this time we have more layers of freedom.

Using the Restored Body House image, write in specific words God has spoken to you on this journey. Feel free to go back to previous journal prompts to see what you wrote along the way. Include as much information as you can, and use the following page for extra processing if you run out of room.

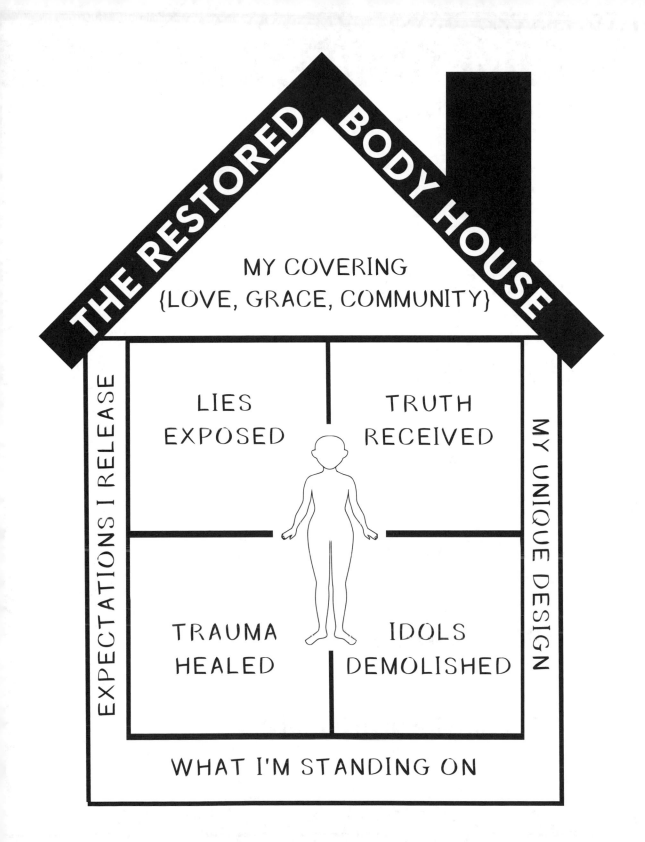

IMAGE RESTORED:

MY COVERING:

LIES EXPOSED:

TRUTH RECEIVED:

TRAUMA HEALED:

IDOLS DEMOLISHED:

EXPECTATIONS I RELEASED:

MY UNIQUE DESIGN:

WHAT I'M STANDING ON:

I leave you with this final charge directly from God:

> Look, I am coming soon! My reward is with me, and I will give to each person according to what they have done. I am the Alpha and the Omega, the First and the Last, the Beginning and the End. (Rev. 22:12–13)

This is our friendly reminder from Jesus that He was here at the beginning, will be there at the end, and is present for everything in between. And He is returning soon. We must refuse to be distracted by this body image battle and instead keep our eyes focused on Him. You were born for such a time as this, my beautiful sisters.

Jesus is the main character in this book on body image. If you don't know Him, some of the principles here won't make sense. I believe you are reading this book because the Holy Spirit is drawing you in to give your life to Jesus Christ. It's as simple as saying the prayer below.

Dear God, I know I am a sinner. Please forgive me for all my sins. I receive Jesus as my Lord and my Savior. Thank you, Jesus, for saving me. In Jesus name, amen.

Acknowledgments

How does one begin to thank everyone who played a role in bringing this book to life?

Let's start with Jesus, the lead role in this entire book.

Jesus, thank You for showing up every time I sat down to write. You pulled Your chair up and You guided me every step of the way. But most of all, thank You for walking me to freedom in my own body image journey. You have always been the only answer.

To Matt, my amazing husband: You are the second-most-talked-about person in this book, right after Jesus. You have loved me as Christ loves the church. It's that love that has brought me freedom and hope. When we got married almost twenty years ago, you saw a fearless woman within, and you have been calling me out and up ever since. Thank you for loving and supporting me unconditionally. I will never forget all the moments in writing this book that you spoke life over me, prayed for me, or did your best at making a meal for our family. You are my rock.

To my beautiful children, Ellie, Olivia, and Zeke: I wrote this book for you. Ellie and Olivia, may you be women who carry this message to your generation. Zeke, may you grow up to be a man of God, just like your daddy. Thank you for believing in Mom as I took time out of our family's schedule to write this book. I couldn't have done it without you.

To my faith-filled parents, Bill and Linda Goldner: You raised me from a young age to stand firmly on the Word of God. While I did stray, I came back to what you taught me about God when I was just a child. You have both always believed in me even when

I didn't believe in myself. Thank you for the lineage of faith you gave me that I now get to pass on to my children and their children's children.

To my literary agent, Jevon Bolden of Embolden Media: From the moment I met you at the Declare Conference, I knew God had brought us together. Thank you for calling out the books within me. Thank you for words of encouragement when I wanted to quit. Thank you for being my Mordecai.

To Susan McPherson at David C Cook: Thank you for believing in me and this project. You have the gift of taking a good idea and making it great. Your peaceful presence made it a joy to work on this project.

To the entire David C Cook/Esther Press family: Thank you for countless hours of editing, brainstorming, marketing, and energy to get this project launched. I asked the Lord to give me a team to support me, and He went above and beyond with you. It's been a blast.

To my developmental editor, Julie Cantrell: God knew I needed a grace-filled woman like you on my first book. You could always sense my fear and call it out so it didn't linger. You challenged me to tighten and soften my writing. You have been a godsend, and I am forever grateful for you.

To my graduate school professor and friend, Dr. Linda Hoover: Thank you for everything you poured into me in school and beyond. Your wisdom has made me a better counselor. Thank you for poring over the pages of this manuscript and for sharing your tips throughout the book. I am grateful for you.

To my LPC Associate supervisor, Dr. Mary Dainty: Thank you for challenging me to be an ethical and wise counselor. Thank you also for being one of the first to read the manuscript and give feedback on how to improve it. But most of all, thank you for the final words you said to me when I was getting caught up in fear and perfectionism in writing the book. Those words helped me release control to God and trust that what was here was exactly what God intended, no more and no less.

To my graduate school professor, Dr. Shannon Crawford: Thank you for teaching me how to be in tune with the Holy Spirit as a therapist. Thank you for the insight you shared in the Therapist Thoughts throughout this book. Your wisdom and discernment are a gift!

To my writing coach, Nika Maples: Thank you for coaching me every step of the way. Our sessions were always exactly what my heart needed to keep writing. I will forever cherish our time together working on this project. Because of you, I took new territory.

To my artistic friend, Michelle Acker: Thank you for designing the beautiful coloring pages throughout this book. Thank you for giggling with me when my soul needed a good laugh. And thank you for reminding me to trust the process. You are a gift.

To my siblings, Jenny, Becky, Caleb, and Sarah: Thank you for leading me well through life. I learned much from all of you. Who would have thought this baby of the family would grow up to be an author and speaker?! That's because of all of you pouring into me and being my biggest fans.

To my uncle Robert and aunt Debbie Morris: Thank you for all you have poured into me over the years. From watching you both write multiple books to sitting under your teachings at church. You have both planted seeds in my life that are blooming. Robert, I will never forget what you told me when I set out to write a book: "Success is obedience." That wisdom has carried me through this journey.

To Grandpa Morris: Thank you for being like a father to me. You have come alongside and taught me about homes, but most importantly, about life. You have supported and loved me well.

To my in-laws, Paul, Nanci, and Debbie: Thank you for taking me into your family like I was one of your own when I married Matt. I have felt nothing but love and support from you all.

To my Declare life group—Eryn, Michelle, Jen, Kristin, and Anne: Thank you for being with me every step of the way on this publishing journey. From conferences to late-night hotel-room chats to our never-ending Voxer messages, you all have been with me through the good, the bad, and everything in between.

To my *Real Talk with Rachael* podcast listeners: First of all, thank you for putting up with me for the last two years talking about this book I am writing. You all have been troopers. But most of all, thank you for showing up every single week not just to listen but to engage in authentic community. The show continues to grow not because of me but because of the real community that is taking place. That's all you. Thank you.

To my body-image-book warriors group: Thank you for raising your hands long before the book released and saying, "Yes, I want to be a part of this movement!" Your feedback and presence have been priceless.

To you, dear reader: Thank you for showing up. You may not know me in real life, yet you trusted me to be your guide. I pray the Holy Spirit knit our hearts together on this journey. This is just the beginning. Thank you for saying yes to the call!

Notes

Introduction: An Inside-Out Approach to Body Image

1. Jessica R. Kusina and Julie J. Exline, "Perceived Attachment to God Relates to Body Appreciation: Mediating Roles of Self-Compassion, Sanctification of the Body, and Contingencies of Self-Worth," *Mental Health, Religion & Culture* 24, no. 10 (2021): 1050–71, doi.org/10.1080/13674676.2021.1995345.

Chapter 1: Choose a Building Site

1. See Jayde A. M. Flett et al., "Sharpen Your Pencils: Preliminary Evidence That Adult Coloring Reduces Depressive Symptoms and Anxiety," *Creativity Research Journal* 29, no. 4 (2017): 409–16, doi.org/10.1080/10400419.2017.1376505.

Chapter 6: Hidden Hurt in the Closet

1. Lee Kneipp, Kathryn Kelly, and Inessa Wise, "Trauma Symptoms as Predisposing Factors for Body Image Distortion," *Individual Differences Research* 9, no. 3 (2011): 126–37.

2. Francine Shapiro, *Eye Movement Desensitization and Reprocessing (EMDR) Therapy: Basic Principles, Protocols, and Procedures*, 3rd ed. (New York: Guilford, 2018), 39.

3. Jon Chasteen, *Half the Battle: Healing Your Hidden Hurts* (Murphys, CA: Gateway, 2020), 16.

4. See Abby Perry, "Did Jesus Experience Trauma? Experts Say 'Yes,'" *CT Creative Studio*, December 13, 2021, www.christianitytoday.com/partners/gloo/did-jesus-experience-trauma-experts-say-yes.html.

5. Diane Langberg, *Suffering and the Heart of God: How Trauma Destroys and Christ Restores* (Greensboro, NC: New Growth, 2015), 74.

6. Langberg, *Suffering and the Heart of God,* 74.

Chapter 7: Thoughts Are the Foreman

1. Joyce Meyer, *Battlefield of the Mind: Winning the Battle in Your Mind*, rev. ed. (New York: Warner Faith, 2002).

2. "The Cognitive Triangle," Therapist Aid, accessed June 9, 2022, www.therapistaid.com/therapy-worksheet/cbt-triangle/cbt/none.

Chapter 8: The Creaky Floorboards

1. See Robert Plutchik, *Emotion: Theory, Research, and Experience,* vol. 1, *Theories of Emotion* (New York: Academic, 1980).

Chapter 9: When Building Is Delayed

1. "What Is Orthorexia Nervosa: Symptoms, Causes, and Complications," Center for Discovery Eating Disorder Treatment, accessed June 10, 2022, https://centerfordiscovery.com/conditions/orthorexia.

Unit 3 Counselor's Cornerstone

1. Cognitive Behavior Therapy (CBT) was developed by Dr. Aaron T. Beck in the 1960s and has proven to be an effective approach to mental health.

Chapter 10: Decorating with Idols

1. J. Swanson, *Dictionary of Biblical Languages with Semantic Domains: Hebrew (Old Testament),* electronic ed. (Oak Harbor, WA: Logos Research Systems, 1997).

Chapter 11: The House Next Door

1. Andy Stanley, *Enemies of the Heart: Breaking Free from the Four Emotions That Control You*, repr. ed. (Colorado Springs: Multnomah Books, 2011), 171.

Chapter 12: Moldy Motives

1. "Eve," Logos Bible Software, Faithlife, accessed July 12, 2022.

Chapter 14: Break the Alarm Cycle

1. Walter Bauer, *A Greek-English Lexicon of the New Testament and Other Early Christian Literature,* rev. and ed. Frederick William Danker, 3rd ed. (Chicago: University of Chicago Press, 2000), 65.

Chapter 15: The Only One on the Block

1. *Merriam-Webster*, s.v. "body image," accessed July 1, 2022, www.merriam-webster.com/medical/body%20image.

2. *Lexico*, s.v. "subjective," accessed July 1, 2022, www.lexico.com/en/definition/subjective.

Chapter 17: God's Grace and Jesus' Face

1. A. B. Luter Jr., " Grace*,"* in *Dictionary of Paul and His Letters,* ed. Gerald F. Hawthorne, Ralph P. Martin, and Daniel G. Reid (Downers Grove, IL: InterVarsity, 1993), 372.

2. Lexico Powered by Oxford, s.v. "favor," accessed June 14, 2022, www.lexico.com/en/definition/favor.

Chapter 18: Find Your Body Image Neighborhood

1. R. W. Wall, "*Community: New Testament*," in *The Anchor Yale Bible Dictionary,* vol. 1, A–C (New York: Doubleday, 1992), 1103.

2. *Merriam-Webster*, s.v. "yoke," accessed June 14, 2022, www.merriam-webster.com/dictionary/yoke.

Resources

Eating Disorder Overview

Body dysmorphia (a distorted body image) and eating disorders often are found together. While this is not a book on the treatment of eating disorders, it is worth bringing them to awareness. If you suspect that you, or a loved one, have an eating disorder, please seek professional help. I've also provided a brief list of the most common eating disorders listed in the *Diagnostic and Statistical Manual of Mental Disorders, Fifth Edition (DSM-5)*.

Avoidant/Restrictive Food Intake Disorder

An eating or feeding disturbance as manifested by persistent failure to meet appropriate nutritional and/or energy needs associated with one or more of the following criteria: significant weight loss, significant nutritional deficiency, dependence on enteral feeding or oral nutritional supplements, marked interference with psychosocial functioning.

Anorexia Nervosa

Restriction of energy intake relative to requirements, intense fear of gaining weight or of becoming fat, disturbance in the way in which one's body weight or shape is experienced, undue influence of body weight or shape on self-evaluation, or persistent lack of recognition of the seriousness of the current low body weight.

Bulimia Nervosa

Recurrent episodes of binge eating, recurrent inappropriate compensatory behaviors in order to prevent weight gain (laxatives, diuretics, fasting, excessive exercise), self-evaluation unduly influenced by body shape and weight.

Binge Eating Disorder

Recurrent episodes of binge eating. An episode of binge eating is characterized by both of the following: eating, in a discrete period of time, an amount of food that is definitely larger than what most people would eat in a similar period of time; a sense of lack of control over eating during the episode. Episodes must be associated with three or more of the diagnostic criteria listed in the *DSM-5*.

Resources for Trauma:

EMDR International Association: www.emdria.org

American Association of Christian Counselors (AACC): http://aacc.net

National Center on Substance Abuse and Child Welfare: https://ncsacw.samhsa.gov/resources /trauma/trauma-resource-center-websites.aspx

Taking Care of Yourself worksheet: www.nctsn.org/sites/default/files/resources/fact-sheet /taking_care_of_yourself.pdf

The Body Keeps the Score: Brain, Mind, and Body in the Healing of Trauma by Bessel van der Kolk, MD (New York: Penguin, 2015)

Health & Wellness:

BBC Health: www.backbodyclinic.com

Counseling Services with Rachael: www.rachaelgilbert.com/counseling

Revelation Wellness: www.revelationwellness.org